The California Poem

Eleni Sikelianos

Coffee House Press
2004

Photos on pages 144 and 154 courtesy of the Bancroft Library, University of California, Berkeley.

Coffee House Press books are available to the trade through our primary distributor, Consortium Book Sales & Distribution, 1045 Westgate Drive, Saint Paul, MN 55114. For personal orders, catalogs, or other information, write to: Coffee House Press, 27 North Fourth Street, Suite 400, Minneapolis, MN 55401.

Coffee House Press is a nonprofit literary publishing house. Support from private foundations, corporate giving programs, government programs, and generous individuals help make the publication of our books possible. We gratefully acknowledge their support in detail in the back of this book.

LIBRARY OF CONGRESS
CATALOGING-IN-PUBLICATION DATA

Sikelianos, Eleni
The California poem / Eleni Sikelianos.
p. cm.
ISBN 1-56689-162-0 (alk. paper)
1. California—Poetry. I. Title.
PS3569.I4128C35 2004
811'.54--dc22
2004012788

ACKNOWLEDGMENTS

Many thanks to the generous editors of the following anthologies, journals, and projects in print and online, where portions of this poem first appeared:

Accurate Key, American Letters & Commentary, Beyond Baroque, Blue Fifth, Bombay Gin, Booglit, Cento, Chicago Review, Conjunctions, The Denver Quarterly, Doubleroom, Ecopoetics, Estuaire (Canada), *Fence, How2, Ixnay, Jacket, KultureFlash, Marks, Medana Days of Poetry & Wine Anthology* (Slovenia), *New American Writing, No, Octopus, Plagio* (Chile), *plan b* (Mexico / U.S.), *Radical Society, Salt Hill, Shiny, So To Speak, Tool, Under the Influence: Younger Women Poets on the Generations Before Them* (Wesleyan), and *Verse*.

Portions of *The California Poem* were used for the film *The Dream of the City*, by Peter Bil, and in a collaborative screening / performance at The Kitchen.

The author wishes to express her gratitude to Yaddo for time to work on this poem.

I would like to thank all the dear friends, family, and colleagues who offered help and support in the process of this poem over the past seven years. They include Brenda Coultas, Caroline Crumpacker, Marcella Durand, Jen Hofer, Sophie Jasson Holt, Garrett Kalleberg, Jonathan Skinner, Anne Waldman, Jo Ann Wasserman, and Joshua Beckman. There will never be a big enough thanks for Laird Hunt, king of the animals in our backyard. Many thanks to Chris Fish, the big cheese, to Linda Koutsky, and to Allan, especially for buying the Berkeley font. And to the artists who made work specifically for this poem: Brenda Coultas, Nancy Davidson, Lorna Hunt, and Isabelle Pelissier; to those who agreed to have their work included: Peter Cole and Merle Porter (permission kindly granted by his widow, Bessie Porter); and to Daron Mueller for providing the Yucca postcard. And to my mother, Elayne, who helped foster my curiosity about the world and its five Kingdoms: Animalia, Protoctista, Plantae, Fungi, and Monera.

for all the echinoderms and dinoflagellates

Melons and plums and peaches, eating and drinking, and the bugle, all the day long. These are the glorious occupations that engross a proud and thinking being, running [t]his race of preparation for the eternal world.

—RWE

Know then, that, on the right hand of the Indies, there is an island called California, very close to the side of the Terrestrial Paradise . . . peopled by black women . . . who lived in the fashion of Amazons. Their arms were all of gold, and so was the harness of the wild beasts which they tamed and rode.

When Queen Calafía and her women, [were] armed with that armor of gold, all adorned with the most precious stones, which are to be found in the island of California like stones of the field for their abundance . . . they caused so much injury . . . that it may cause you equal pleasure . . .

—GARCIA ORDÓÑEZ DE MONTALVO,
Las Sergas de Esplandián

Prologue

Let me tell you of my cat-o-nines cosmovision.

After the last light on clouds, darkness came laying over the known world
with a sick at heart that could only be carved out of gold & cured
           with $35 worth of history
Hunger unhinged the doors, hypertension in the trees

Hi-summer, lo-summer, waiting for golden hordes of killer bees; smoking holes, haloes
                  on copper mines

When I looked up it had already changed again—
No more fair, no flaxen clouds:

While the light lingers in layers on high
deserty lands lie in the dark   smoothed floor that the night has seen
Dipping my toes in the Pacific off the edge of—
Tell, what lurks at the boundaries

Scattered across Precambrian rock: spent shot-
         gun cartridges, bullet-
                  flown bottles
                      truckle, the Glass
           Factory at Lizard's Mouth shatter

                  shatters birds   *tibiotarsus, furcula*

Evel Knieval jumped the Snake River Gorge; we saw
General Patton's path
in Mojave dust, modern man
run amok in the desert

                 Might our lands lift off
                        the pale
              face of the earth & float
                     away, a
             glittery sheet,
                   Ghost,
             lift up in us some
                   shiver   should wastelands
            arouse themselves out of dumb
                   stupor

So we elaborated our peninsula out past the resort Town of Tijuana; mating
turtles mistook the lights of Cancún
for the moon, malls made a language
        "to eat up
           available reality"

"By now the dream is falling in on itself . . .
Or someone is dismantling it . . ."

Now: to let go what we knew
to not be tight, but
toney; to find a world, a word
we didn't know

. . . concentrate on the consciousness
the sea comes out of

—FH

I dreamt of a land of water:

•

I woke with those chords in my head, and it was off like a soft explosion.

—JA

I want to tell you about the dream. The California is a paradise lake with colorful animals dream.
The when I go back to my homeland California is a paradise I am happy for you dream

We were going ever so through the dusty eucalyptus the dusty eucalyptus & shadow road in the
"opposite of blindness" & "relinquished speech"

The lake is to the left. On one side, a tall Pink bird invented by space and time called

Flamingo, & there, other small & medium birds shiny & loose
with pockets of Geryon-ash-gold What can be lit I'll light that I'll light that for you dream

a kissing everything good-bye in the ballad's hide & an eye

of spit

a thoin gutterful of vowels
out of the battery & ground

in the teeth, death
in the bush, 2 in the hand

in the nape of the napalm of sun-shore-sun I am an orphan! dream

. . . . . . Who was counting the ribs
in my grandfather's ships? My Fist vs. Coastal

margins of coconut novelties which recede
and advance upon the shelf like a carved humidor army, Razor
clams, diatoms, wentletraps, drifting

away from the dream of California

which is dust & light & dust

being tossed in the white

chenille

blanket beside the low white stucco barracks
with roosters between the houses scratching at the dust of light of the dream

thorny and antic
shapes as tall as a house sticking up out of the desert part
of California   tiny flowers frozen in the tips   Needles
birthed a poet named Alice and goat-weed

This poem
is therein, in my dream of Death
Valley, cakey layers of land, gloss of gloss
Angeles & Inyo County is just

dusty in the bus station at the cold night shifting
from foot to foot in 1973. Tumbleweeds
go by.

In my sleeping nostalgia for *The Streets*
of San Francisco dream like seeing Michael
Douglas in an elevator in
California (not
that satisfying), or
my dream of a saguaro flower weather or California in the shape
of Karl Malden's nose as it appears
in *One-eyed Jacks*.

In California we don't say bodega except
for the bay, we say
market, which is what
it is. We don't say buttercup
we say butter box or butter cut. If you say margarine, we bodacious
we don't say you be we say I is
In California, fire hydrant is a way to say freeway which in turn turns to freely allie All ye
in come free into dusk motes

at Lake of our Lady, etc., by the seashore & my right hand very close to the Earthly Paradise California
named for a tribe
of Ladies with Big Feet, Rose Bowl
football & the black hole
of Livermore where the flames and the tripods expired. It is

all of New York, New England,
Pennsylvania, & New Jersey combined.

Laugh for the eucalyptus as an object of pity
The truth of Georgia is not to be found here in sushi dinners

but there is the dirt bike parade
in the mud behind subdivision A-3, Santa Maria,
Camarillo, & so on, near the lemon groves both beautiful & useful behind
the funnyfarm & more lemon groves. My grandmother's ranch
was a small pit stop inside a lemon seed. My grandmother's gas station was

two concrete slabs laid out in the Mojave. Her hair
a tumbleweed sprayed in the shape of a Kelp Limpet, Gilded Turban, & the lemon
leaves will brush one's head, & the spiderwebs are fresh & dewy, the mouse turds can be found under
the chaparral. My grandmother spends weekends in ghost towns looking for scorpions to cast
in lucite. She collects California rocks, for she is a rockhound, and she collects California rattlesnakes,
for she is a tailhound, and she will open a health-food store and sell frozen buffalo meat for this is
California and she will embezzle money from the local paper and live in a trailer plunked in the
middle of the sands with every salvageable imaginable thing from the shores
of the unshored Inyokern   a goat named Angel   guppies   her ladies in diners   geodes
cracked open at the door

In the deadyard at Dolores crumbling into dust & light is California and California's
variegated surface forgets that dust which came
to bequeath them space & light, nudibranchs did I
say Cachuma's foot
prints in the ashy mud of the bones of our forefathers ground
up like pellets did I turn to the bones of mice bones in the coyote fox eagle shit

A spine brought to the whole length of California was laid out like a golden wheel-veil
of cascades of oldest & largest living things and everything was crushed
in a Catherine wheel

At 13, I acquired a good tan in California
to brush with the gods & god squeezers & boring
and smiling compliments so much less
to rake and scratch the character on

as I too was raked along the bottom
feeders & surface
waters like El Niño doing a brody
through our air/hair at the Sunday meeting I was myself a dumb
dog who could not bark

at the sadness of early California, the sado-masos down from the hills and Sadducees, their
desire, denial of everything dead, and the existence of angels;

California and Sadie Hawkins;

& its meadows associated with human folly, its airs of superiority, knowing
the it and what
it is.

And the echinoderms[i] give up
their radial symmetry. The laughable echinoderms moving back
toward bilaterality like drunken teens

California in the lights of the trees
my hedon eden I rushed
to California with my eyes
closed. Ron or Bill or George or John or Sam, our president was there, fire rushed
down his snout like a dining rage & through
the pinelands of Banana Road, like three light fingers making waste across the ice lakes of Jupiter's
cow moon, Io.

From the center of rice I do remember California
stitched up twice
in my memory of sleeveless shirts &
Ocean A, D or Q
behind the not tall buildings

       I know nothing of Northern
North California therefore
there is none, Eureka, Arcata, etc., yet I
would like to sell [you] [send] you California
& its industrial wastelands, its Crips
& Bloods, the
ACTION! CAMERA! and fully-armed cactus. Each studio is a nation-
state of its own under the cloudless blue
neon & the bright
stucco Draco
of sun
of tile
of bottlebrush
of lovely picture baby
bird-
of-paradise
honeysuckle
yucca
Joshua
Tree, home
of John Steinbeck,
& me

      ⊰

The dental imprint of California
is gravelly, epileptic, spasm
of a sea-borne bungled broken Coastal Range of ridges & spurs with localized names

    parking lots littered of glittering dead dented cadillacs

    scum-fringed greenfingered gully muck silent in its ditch by
    oak of tentacular brow & birds
    shoot up quilling like grapeshot

    my trailer park's in the shady ambrosial arroyo of nothing native
    stands of embryonic eucalyptic bluegums frilling on the ridge &
    tractor dust like a dress for us
    Everybody's halfcracked with halfteeth missing and ideas of almost-functioning

    shipping & receiving depts. near the train tracks collide, hillsides
    scrubbed in wild brighting mustard

    unknown modes of road wind back the black hot gila monster tarmac beading up into ripped hills

    pinioned slats & sacks stacked up against
    mudslides, the night-

    boxed lemons loaded into truck-backs in the dark by brown bodiless hands

pop-eyed bushes rush out of banked ditches, give toothless speeches on
the nasturtium's flaming clump that chomps hills to fire, reddened eyes of

those who walk slow or dogged
through tract house streets under sunlight, their
not-mysterious lives

Our hours
our long hours

in dormant crooks in cool canyons lazily drumming along the pipelined coast
We've roamed these

underpasses in our underpants & frontage roads by bicycle with blownout
tire in flipflops or running shoes

my gritty California registry of big trees *whoah!* harnessing hamstrung slugs onto the waterbugs'
shadows, dark daisies skittering
        along the bottom rocks

the low humming bird of trains in the night like a lion with a harmonium
in its throat
running
        in its soft clickety-clack socked tracks
                along the sea

all the vatos drip inky
tears down to fingertips
dark dolphins slip
down, cambered backs in

& out of view

> falling
> headfirst toward
> a human race
> who's toiled, tailed
> by the tiny bones
> that float unknown
> to the body:
> rage, sadness, dismay

Angela, Barbara Dee,

> The Monterey pines are high
> & dark & you are stuck in jail
> Hand me   the black
> prison phone   Tell them
> all chola girls to be set free

Hacienda Liquor Mart in the kicking dust / I'm
riding a train in the equestrian version of the dream all over your green campus sloping up
toward SLOtown where the horses' torsos play ball

> *Orale pues*
>> Oracle Pass foretold:

> *Muchachas, muchachos*, my father will not
> make his drug connection in the night & you
> will live in limos in blue plastic-covered parking lots   Night
> will not manage to mess up your language

ever-renewable in the new age—old rage—rocks at the train—
from the projects
by the recycling heap
where I sent my head
my empties
of milk to bed
this morning

Little arches just up from the concreted riverbed said
we can walk through the hollow
under the freeway unlit, free

to walk in the dark all night & all day

My tag is Rotn Red
Bitch, my bungalow is beach

The beautiful grown ground
my view from-the-diamond view
of a black crow slicing
tree to tree

geodesic creosote
skeleton subdivision the bones
        thrown up pine window to look
                upon pine window

We are free to move about
                                without bodies before

the quiet velvet of cars in the night before

the velvet ears of helper rabbits

but I want my party to be waiting for me wherever I go

At the depot my people, my party
are not waiting for me. At Union Station, everybody's got a lump
or a bruise & a limp, & they all need $5.75 to get
to Oceanside.

California, where the car brakes never work and I always roll
                                through stop signs, into the gaps

of glowing green lights through the trees

There are things that keep us
from work and school: the rain, or each husband
who comes home with a 60"-screen color TV

"which has brought me here
to the gold of all my wishing"
to give an account of our first ages,
and of all the great events which happened
in the infancy of the world when

having no tan to work on I was
working on my self, *shiny shiny*

California
was my glistening chapel
Westminster Cathedral, gothic
beach scenes to the west

Memory can be anyone's shimmering
Albion, bathyspheric hellhole hideout *trop sévère*
in such a book of sun I like too much

liken it to the apathy of opposite collaborations
with Carmathian mortality
sifting spiritual liquids filled with less than these colors
into microfine powders & let them drift
through air, with the words
      red through red
            blue through blue

into the kingdoms of the western rimlands
in the crack up of the old orders
the winged sea towers our coastal artists drew
The Chief of the House, Keeper of the Chalk, slips off
my hereditary admiralship of Ocean Sea
in a swarm a storm, my restless
my rootless people
just as a bird is homeless
I am homeless too

dream music with holes in it

At the bottom of the sky, thinking
curves space, makes
rocks look
rubber; my eyes
cared about color, not
heat; my heart, however
cared about heat. The same story turns

to another end when I said

They are carving me into a shape now, maybe a boat, now
I am licking a frozen stone. This is how the

California

is thawed from its cryogenic state, born
from a divinely created eater of granite   in my universal soul-fire-Heraclitus   with a face
made of wood   combustible   smile   carved

right in   back made of rocks
                                precipice, spine made of flint
                                        igneous trunk
        at the collision of ardent clouds, head formed
                                my reefy iliac crest   bursting

                    into flame like burning
seas sprung from the blood like

tear a live [California] apart with your teeth

Strip it

to its animal / vegetable / mineral husk

to its last residuum;
or other ways to make a world, like:

putting honey on a fly's wings to deepen the buzzing
trimming a bird's wings to deepen the buzzing
make seaside cockroaches with human faces

A narrow strip between low tide and shoreline where sands and rocks are often wet and damp; where reefs and rocks extend from shore.
Surf grasses & sea lettuce
Sandpiper, Wandering Tattler, Heermann's & Western Gull
a crab, a barnacle, beach flea, an isopod, some beach hopper

Q: California—could I go and see it if I wanted to?

A: Yes, if you have perspectives.

Q: Could anybody see it?

A: Anyone, if they have glasses. And *can* see . . .

Q: And *can* see . . . ?

— Yes.

— Even if you yourself have never seen it?

— Yes . . . and *can* read. Can read the way it slides into sugar. It's been a skin, in words, "war" branded into the lips, and buildings built, and bad land slid right into the sea—it slid yesterday, a little, today.

— Can you see it sliding then?

— In their American eyefolds they carry half the secret primer for pulling up bone prisms

      & cover their coast with gold

      where birds

      where birds fly for words

      and we can drive some stones into the ground and make a million

— But *can* you see it *sliding?*

— Into the sea, and can pay for it. If you can read the way most people are kept separate there. They can't tell you what time of day it is, what season, what war or year. They slide and get dissolved and will rise up again.

— Are you saying in California it's grim?

A: It's grim in the dim light of rebar covering the coast. In the hotels' wheels covering the sea. The quaint docks lit up for the traveler, the boardwalks for snapping holiday photos, muscle men made to kick quicksand, back-to-nature quonset huts, footprints of alfalfa seed liquid kafka diets, flotation chambers, guru warlords, gunnysacks, and sand between your knees . . . it's funny there—it's grim.

Then they cut the rope
and set the boat adrift.

Fair Coast in the country of the
otters make offers
& other things
touched upon in a by-
clause of the oracle, fate
like a satrap saddling hills to
look in to. "See see the world's
incarnate," See,
my Pantyocracy was invented
in intensities of blue

and if I can stand, I can
stand it, a corpus walking
by familiar demonstration, my tough
walk-up

What, sailor?

I can stand therefore
I can, where is
a probable deck
without stars above the
jacuzzi. Down from the cliff, I stick
my fingers

into sea anemones with a finger that if
left too long will turn

to bone My patterned flesh so
variable, barbaric, sometimes ecstatic. So you go

on an idealistic binge, a person
who was thinking this thought or that
          in the evening's drift . . .
where storms gather outside the night-
time window's
          frame & far out
at sea . . .   .
. .   . .
. .   . . If the clouds are not moving, the window
from the house seems frozen, but we know waves
may still be knitting out in places we cannot see . . . . . .

          —Benthic cave & crevice, cryptic abyss, tongued blue

                                                            holes
     in softened consonants between sad & saditty; jugular

and roughed-up
thought, I turn to you, of you
frying potatoes
in a football helmet, sagittal
arrows dividing the skull, beads
of light on your chin catching
light—that is, water, "the ghostly poles known
to the body"

I know what I am for awake
A reminiscence sing
(I remember food stamps and funny looks in checkout lines)

How does a blind girl learn to strut?
I remember every minute being over-lived
You better ask your master who's her hair
(Her hair is master of her head)
("The neck is dropped deeper into the body")
I remember looking into nighttime bedrooms where strangers
       watched TV in underwear, faces bathed in blue
           denotative light

      —Was that decorative?

I remember a man in a leotard tossing a medicine ball & pulling boats
between his teeth, he made us
drink smoothies & carrot juice; his name
was Jack LaLane

For these

are the researches of Eleni, of melatonin patches
between the Channel Islands in whose floating hands I
invisibilize my blackness illuminate
of the green geometry (transepting grass upon grasses)
                      Island, hands of land, come
quick, come back
to haunt the grayer hours; snatch back
that diamonda minute I tried to slip between

I find no synonym for hour but house
no analogue for dark but light
no iguanodon but time, so

a late hour and wine are able to do as much as when I laugh there is no evil
angel but Love but when I laugh the brontosaurus
laughs with me

And just as internal summer shall heal or hinder Pindar
& hands degenerate into hands

so the world was very guilty of such a thing—fast
& loose flowers, dark rafts

floating out over dark water
roots of my hand on a sleeping forehead, it's weird

> how solid,
> how deep
> is sleep
> how sleeping is
> s[p]oiled by sleepers

       How can I dream right in the subway anywhere else, with dead
plastic bags, I can't remember even my good
dream from the good
bed where the word for
words come
into my head. How can you know what you really think if you can't
say what you really think I can't think In
California you can't think. There, "reverence is a kind of fear" just as Hang
Ten is a kind of shorts you wear.

It seemed to me that it was most expedient to bring my conduct
into harmony with the ideas of those with whom I should have to
live . . .

—Descartes

but since I / they hardly had any ideas, I found myself idea-less,
adrift . . .

To travel the deeps of air with no fear, my wagoneer

the Magellanic Clouds
are idle & gray & I am growing
a wooden spoon of verse to stir words into thoughts like things; the arthropodic
aquatic mandibulates are moving
delicately across the surface soils, there is no point

in going to the mat, no point
in going to starry Texas again, no point, the cyanometer, for measuring
intensities of blue, no point
to soliloquize upon the table, in having a soul
for a body (Having no heart to show, she shows her teeth)
            (—Wrestle the damn dream down!)

        And I remember when I'm sleeping, that's objects floating
through space, the moving room floating toward night, come
terror me, dark, the way
I was terrored, Camino del Sur: It was carpets and green, square, and low
and had no dirt, love, until the blackness in back, and thus repeated
a bumping parking lot right up to the weeds. The fields
there have been eliminated, therefore I remove green
to a faraway place till green melts out of the world
of any other place

       Move five blocks toward the water, there is laced
coral on the hem
of a soft & feathery dress; a skirt skirted
in nettle hair triggers, deadly batteries of cardiotoxic nematocysts, the colonial
animals fasten themselves to the bottom
of the sea where hair
waves, I have not

remembered to mention the darkest of series the place where I was thinking
       California
or the almonds at Mycenae sleeping
trees under the sleepy ground, their light strings dangling dream of the fixed
trees of all Mars and all Marin; mariner, my voice is
tangled there where the phone lines tangle with the sea

The child is named Left Over Arms & Legs
She Who Has Something Strapped To Her Back
She Who Can't Sleep

      Can you claim responsibility for this human cargo?

The tone is important: "Lay down
your gun"

      Does your skirt still light up? Is it
      aflame?

Yo, thou thouest

little bird in the earth black back
of the car   —   Oh, what's this — the
car is an earth! the bird is a self! the
mask is human!   & shows the
insuperable nest next to the second
ago, shattered, saying, "What, friend?" "What
precision" "What art" in proper names we repeat
tea habits over complex
centuries in   gold = discovery,   gold =
luminosity, gold = grief, greed, the
killer at the back of the sea, say, says
words do describe my aversion to drag rag-
dolls down to the river, a river
sibling over the middle waters

It cleans "you"

Now I'm planning on not being that person that I was

So you, so you go
        toward the music, human

It was distant & luminous beyond
an 8-year-old of my position to move across
it down toward the sea.
            the sea.   or
        that is how I remember it, what
        I remember I believed

It ended on the beach

with a hulk

of turquoise color, birds

lost among the dead

glided on those burning waters,
the country of ~~Red~~ Daylight

is falling
& fell upon

A silent land across which no animal moved & no animal made a sound
The earth fell   in folds
   & wrinkles into ditches, a shield of granite
over Hudson Bay, soft-bodied animals   slipped in the tide

The great tribes
of armored arthropods stepped forth, ghost crabs sped along beaches

   fish, stream-molded by Silurian rivers; we invented
mechanical ears & eyes

Soon cattle & their young corresponded
to the affections of the natural mind

   Begin with a homophone, move
   through numbers, animals & rocks participated
   in the inventions of language[ii]
   (from the snapping of twigs
   we learned k's and t's)

& two-wingèd creatures, according to their species,
to my two minds; is why
my birds
fly with words
one wing for each
hemisphere to create

the worlds
by naming:
first girl looked in the river, saw her face
& soon made a watery mirror of the world, bilateral,[iii] asymmetrical

I name it

and name it
in each tiny eye
of the cell
where the cytochrome
drinks language
a blue wave of color
washes the body
[new body, born veins]

we will be edged in ink
and drenched in ink
and clogged and drowned in ink
powdery figments of all that we are and say and do   do not see

Night pushes through
the walls of a first flower,
wells up in the throat:
ink bottle choked, first fumes

and seed scatters
the gene, teeth splayed
bright on midnight now
each cell has a brain
each color a shifting code

I trade this chrome
for that chromosome
late liquids seep
and all colors that first flower contained
at its edges (membranes)
weep

(Hollywood, La Brea)
*(Man moves in; animals
and plants move out)*

Ages-extinct fires near tiny dragon-headed lakes
Chewing the fat fire-side & touching up a wooly mammoth, mastodon,
mini-horses, chasing
ground sloths the size of tanks   Giant shining
armadillo roll over   (silver wheels crushing tender grasses)
    Edentata belonging to the (inhabited) Earth, edacious at the tooth of Time
            nibbling some sweet thing, fiery
    Hymenoptera edulcorated by their history with men

Told jokes in the clean-flaked keen-flint
glowing coal ice-age night-wind
roared songs at hapless herbivores high moon near wet
meadow sedge

& cut across the cordilleras, rainwater sluicing down
mountainsides made whole new mesas, highlands thrown up

They made several suns & destroyed them
They made humans but destroyed them
They were looking for the right world
Was this the 5th California?
They let the demented Spanish invade, they kept

               the Spanish, kept
               the orange tree, abalone, they kept
Jayne Mansfield & destroyed her

They had no
star clock clucking
out the night hours

no way to track the ragged lights at the edges of towns

but the opossum god of all opossums
carrying corn in its pouch to feed peripheral citizens

& we could see
the parts inside the contours of the body

the dreams of liberation for yoginis of average capacities
the intricate irrigation canals covering Mars
the luminosity in the known moment before death
All that happened in the history books, all

the humans you've ever heard of or met
happened here, he said, pointing
to a little sandbox with a bone-tool, this
talking thinking meat, it
happened

on a wide & fat map
that encompassed California
where we dumped shit into the sea at West

or East, on this narrowing-in-the-middle map, belted
with cords dangling from Indiana, Ohio

I traveled here on a coal barge
in an earlier era with
winding roads through backwoods towns & canopies of trees

I sang their songs in night
cellars & concert taverns, every candy-ass
put-the-hawk-on-you in the shape
of Heaven & Hell, and other human capacities

I might find "occasion to
sing war & perfect soldiers"—
the war that wages over the
face of the Earth, against
every edible turtle &
movable tree, the tyranny
of money

Wearied at last of watching, they danced again, this time on the lower rim of the earth where the river meets the sea. Keeping to the rim, they turned their backs to the river, dancing away from the Nom-ti-pom toward the north. The time of the dead leaves was past. The fog moon came and went, and it was already the time of the mud moon and of frosts. They saw all about them storms and rain and floods, but there on the lower rim of the earth there were no storms, and they continued to dance along its sometimes rocky, sometimes sandy shore.

—"Dance Mad," as told by the Wintu (Sacramento Valley), *The Inland Whale*

Do not forget this list

My oceanaria in occulting light

Ocean tramps of bulk & krill: whales (™ the name) arrayed in beauteous blue

My arthropod's palpers in full earthly paradise

The libro d'oro of palmyra palms, a frond's great Syriac history

Pentecostal pit-vipers making J-tracks across the sand

Mexican jumping beans 99¢[iv]

Hammering diamondbacks with shovels & saving the fangs

Happy eukaryotes called in aid: my Paraclete, come please me / with

Anti-g clothes for my poem, an accelerating thing

Anti-g clothes for all the family of White & Sulphur sucking nectars not speed:
     Sleepy Orange, Alfalfa, Cloudless Sulphur, Cabbage White

California Dogface, eating False Indigo

Sara Orangetip, kiss the dark progress of a storm & wet
     your wingtips

Telson my final integument in arachnid armor, arguing with Black Widows
     in ditches trying to bite the ankle-biters
(we mason-jarred the widow and watched her red hourglass X spin, amazed)

Mob rule of toxic monarchs & desert Queens, fiery brushfoots burst forth
    from parti-colored caterpillar feeding on backlot milkweed
        jewelry for a ringfinger

The tobacco hornworm eyed me from a tomato plant, its threatening spike veered north

Instars of my larval life running
    through poison oak & toothed coyote brush, tethered to mountainsides & falling
        for the honied romance of names

Made a dictionary arranged not alphabetically but from heaven to earth: all things
    of the sky go there ↗ all things of the earth ↘

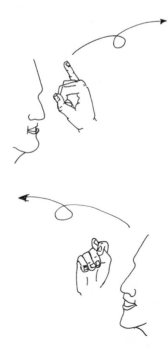

A Simple Lettered Key

  A. With two wings (one pair) ....Flies

AA. With four wings (two pair) ....B or BB

  B. Forewings hard and leathery; without veins ....Beetles

BB. All four wings of equal consistency and veined ....C or CC

  C. Wings covered with tiny scales; mouthparts
modified into a long tube for sucking that is
coiled beneath the head ....Butterflies
and Moths

CC. Wings without scales; clear and membranous ....Ants,
Bees, or Wasps

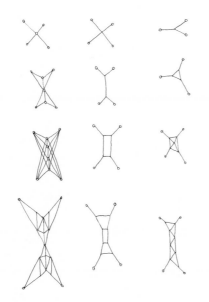

I am sick for my land (home-
land) on buses & in elevators
at Union Square. I am sick
for it in the axis of taxis that run over the dark flattened
gum spots of the East.^v In my TV
arm, my iron leg, in the lazy images of closed-
circuit cameras, sick

for the summer shadows in heedless waters,
islands, mountains, giving in
to hazy sea where lounge a thousand hipsters

In this eastern seaboard state's upended shopping carts on meridians, in frozen freeways
near shallow lakes, gather dockets of historic muck—No
salt-creeks run miles into open air, no deserts crumbling into Death Valley

Be down with that brand of California, for in
foreign CA we have no densely built devil's forest
No evil swarm of suffocating green to tear
hair by hair, no black flies biting
No bower, but a brothel of leaves happily uniting

For did not California elaborate beneath her gown that most essential
sweet and watery matter, as master of the
pentagonal *Oreaster*?

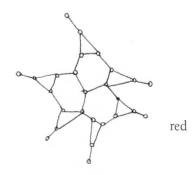

red

It's O.K. here but we don't have any sourgrass
not so many happy lizards in the sun
seaweed sliding back toward licking the sea
sandflies, sandfleas
jogging men nasty naked along the beach & Joakim's oily eucalyptus combusting up toward heaven

I was swimming in the black water under-
neath my breath & then
dragged by the seaweed vines and belts

the water is yellow with sand and ecology, my friends

are being punished by off-duty fathers in tract houses they are not allowed to leave
          after dark

My family is wily, we live in derelict apartments, are government
subsidized, go
everywhere
at night
on shore

Oil rigs out in the water like lighted bird-palace places

In the dream of dying cephalopods

Cuttlefish feathers & things
invented by sound & light like

the Great Spangled Fritillary monarch, and magnitude
of scales, what lies in inner and outer margins of such
wings "that came with soft
alarm, like hurtless light," and the numberous thunder
of veins

Bluebellies in strange arrangement break their tails
in weedy nooses to grow back new ones
Backs bend in the rows between crop-dusted plants, the little singing seeds sting the
fingers & stain them: red, red

Eagle shells crumbling under the eagle's weight croaking at Cachuma Lake

California did not hold its shape
when [the condors] were laid end-to-end
to form a replica of California
with photographs & balsa wood & glue
which was later
beamed to space
(from Big Sur). This message is in regards to
gardens of the sea: graphed
in the scallop's eyes (bright), amid its tentacular
fringe: writ

in fossil guts of hermaphroditic oysters[vi] hanging
out in kitchen middens, a theatre

acted out on land-
masses between bivalves (motory "self-powered
castanets" fluttering

in zig-
zagging arcs) and hungry
bipeds. This heroic

fantasy is set
in an ominous landscape, a dark world that mirrors our watery arms
and legs but not our muscular
hearts

                              Have I been shaped like
                              an animal, god, or
                              have I been good?

Everything I know
occurred in California and everything
I know later, everything I know of California
is shaped like a piece of cardboard
and smells like the black plastic pitch that stretches between Bakersfield & apricots

blue & green & the penny arcade, my dream is just like that:
a thousand miles
long & deep into the otter ice water cliffs

almonds Fresno when I was nearly blond & knees straight
as an arrow & my name
was Dylan-in-the-grass-blue-grass, when my home-
stead read: Mary-of-the-villas
of-the-vocables-of-conches Jalama ice plant and Spanish
mosses

At its Eastern Boundaries of the Ear
Without answer key or blue fig California

at its goldenest gold, brimfullest bright
of citron, sun, when the blazing pollen falls all, all California blooms
pornographic, hysterical flowers Loyal
daughters of the revolution   horses whinnying
up State Street stamp the independence of California into the tarmac Chumash
dancers with fancy feet but
no state.

In *One-eyed Jacks* Marlon Brando and Karl Malden will escape
on steaming ponies, and the beautiful Mexican girl, and roar
into that sleepy village just north of Salinas with its beautiful low Chinese dwarf
cypress in a shady glen & the village is
of Chinese hoteliers, fisher people with gray eyes railroad coolies who bent their
backs & did not break in filmy
VistaVision.

Salinas rises from its
valley like a huge dusty mutt mottled
with lettuce and chemicals not of trash in the state's hallways I want to make you dream this
just as you
made me dream you in a beginning
of bundles and other beginnings
slash
endings.

"Get up you scum-suckin' pig," growls Brando and plays
a wild card.

It was dangerous
to go swimming nightly in the ever-present
oceans, the water slapping
against the rocks massages Mr.
Malden's proboscis like a Nemertean worm gently retiring to sandy tunnels, struggling with
Hercules' Nemean lion in the water's inky womb, black places
in the mind. The nose
is twice as long as the body, sent scuttling into burrows, sometimes it disguises itself
as shoelaces in harbors where anchored
filtering mussels lie
sleepy, it might snarl
into spiraled coils and tangle in knots where Dante walked
in secret chambers
of the human heart, dangerous
waters where pools
dread

The homicides we did not hear of appear again my father's friends disappearing Eddie can you
hear me The chief of police is Irish (says "purr" for "poor") and used to break eggs with you (Eddie
has no teeth) purr Eddie

making 10-pound bags of oatmeal for breakfast, all the food for a month; Eddie is lost; lies
in the land of covalent ditches, culverts where turnpikes meet creeks not shadowed by ceilings nor
thought but the dancing shadow puppets of water bugs cast onto streambeds   his head
in mud near animals hiding
in talus cones—find them by their
eye-shine in the night

Sidewinders and autumn sciroccos. Winos tell stories in the back with their hands. The son comes home from a long trip. The wino opens the car trunk and there is the girlfriend, dead, and the father gets in the car and he drives, he buys a shovel and he drives. He buries her deep in the desert and he never says where. This he does not say to the son, but maybe he buries her somewhere near Soda Lake or Cadiz under the scurry and rasp of things in the desert

"For my part I know of no river called Ocean, and I think that Homer, or one of the other poets,
invented the name" The Sun, therefore, I regard
as the sole
phenomenon

Follow the foot-
prints inside the nerve cell; they lead to a bright
door: tiny patch of memory

a fiery trailer home amidst earlier construction
Action heroes collapsing into dust The bus stops
here; there is no buck in this story, not for this hero
except in purely silver quarters smuggled out of the house in the mouth,[vii] king snakes
caught in jars

Shields are up. Come the
collectors into the vast comma of our tiny trailer. We are collecting
dust. They want money. They want to tell us we are not allowed to live in fields in the black
thorax of the bull-infested land

In this dream I will make you take the train
to *you* dressed up as miles of wooded ocean and coast-
lines with no one on them. You can't see
old people here because of the sunlight.

Earlier, I had my elbow in the yellowest California, we talked
about the coin-shaped trapdoors on gastropods, as the possible versions
of a virgin California slipped away from me
into the geranium, scraggly
nasturtiums on the fire escape. Here in this living-
room there is no sea. Who

cares about the sea?

I do

because the sea
makes us land-like but think
sea-like   because I can only ever think

about things swimming there; *Delphinidae,* which herald love, diligence
and swiftness

(and the constellation delphinus in the sky)

Issuing from the mouth of this animal is a flower: jessant, of a
jerkwater town at the back
of a branch-line train

where runny stars rain by
like eggs, golden
& locked, a hometown is a waiting place, a waiting place is
static inside the heel

I therefore developed longer toes for walking on floating vegetation (*jacanidae*)
the ancient celadon-and-shining agave lining the path all the way down to the sea

In California, we put crystal-clear
marbles in our ears
so we can't hear

the ricochet of neighbors fighting
feet crunching through the underbrush
thumb harps, fiberglass padding being pulled back from drywall

In other hoods they heard
    the jacuzzi cover sliding back
sound of plastic kissing itself off water

just as Agamemnon's shimmering mask
    lying quiet in the secret sweaty chamber
        slides back to reveal the thrill

of blacking out in the lackluster days   Can I sell you this

room of unusual weather
this brain made for pleasure
these deluginous rains of diluvial California crashing
        catywampus through the world

for anything less than storm convergence skyrocket fleamarket rates, water spouts
like one-dimensional phonographs spatting on the horizon will cost a lot . . .

A dull roar falls
on the little white houses stacked up in the trees
a maddened brain made it, in the palatial
                        stucco horatio
                        alger places constructed

in mud
& bunchgrass chumash
once loved

Earth's amorous edifices, Pyramids, TransAmerica, Twin Towers will no longer hold you now
(grab on to vagabondish space)

We soon came to believe
that the world had been made
& we could make it no further

    Listen: who's creating the world
    here, Eleni or opossums?

(It's me against the animals in this)
(Fishes against birds)
(Vermin against the leeches of Zaca Lake)

    Who
    is of more use on the face of the earth, Eleni
    or opossums?

Opossums have
the ears of . . . a ray of light . . .
with no other . . . delicious intentions . . . . . . what
position were we in . . . suffering when . . .
. . . "when clearly intended . . . to be having pleasure" . . .
all that troubled moisture in the brain making

thought is love / not
machine is love / not

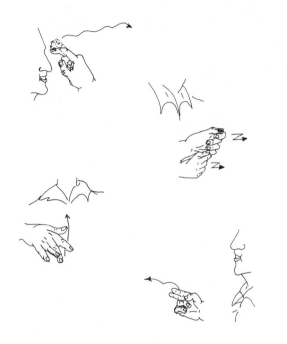

Ah ha ha!
California is opening
the refrigerator door—what's
in there? Avocado,
alfalfa sprouts, and we are laughing our heads off
in Goleta because we just
smoked a lot of pot & don't
have any theories

but obloquies on
L.A., evil
smog-choked city
to the South, like black witchcraft
practiced next door, a rotten
pot *(olla podrida),* of those cities
historically lousy with devils

The politician stands in sunlight, vice
      like an oil swimming
at the surface of his body

All of human history
is lying in the grass, in
nature, there is nothing
we can do to escape it

so just relax, Sybarite, (Symbiont),
and let this melt
from my hand to yours
like tar seepages on the beach
used to caulk gaps in knowing

Of course I am the
messenger of Belief
& Truth

address me as
Gracious & Benign
animal—Ho—not

so? made for
war?
which is as much as to say the heavens
of flame where
all knowledge is contained

whence I might almost entirely
perceive myself in shadows
cast on earth

1) in winterstorms
        sea snails torn
        from shells & washed
        ashore

2)   (\ \ public masturbators made it hard to relax)

3) smoking a doob on Goleta pier near
        the *Salvavidas sauve qui peut*   do not know that language
            spoken here

4)   pinni-
        ped (bear climbed back to sea), black
        stealth bomber will steal your squid with-
                out getting hooked

5) hometown tar on my feet, fog a feathery mask
                / / grayworld
                        did not mask my (often) mood but
                            mirrored it

6) to distinguish between the rush
        of cars / rush
                of sea
            grinding
                    shapes   of the mind

7)   (/ / sea whispers   what at us)

8) Let the musclemen, cowboys die off & the Pacific
    win

thus did he claim to his horse Incitatus and
took off the breastplate he'd looted
from bright Alexander's tumulus; nothing
will teach us
nor tear us past

hybrid fires haunting
unidentified cities,
cosines fluttering like black flies
around the (death) equals sign

even chemical ratios in the clouds
will buzz to make
the rain come down in

white shrouds
around freeway cars, rainwater's
ghosts;   so

those souls & sounds suspended
& hanging in trees
(one per leaf)—umm—I was asking

how to get farthest away
from Heaven, say
cavities of Hell
    but Hell is
at the true
center   in this first
fiery relay
of grace

asked Virgil,

"should we
pillage woods, thick
coverts of game, point
to new-found streams"?

Sylvan Hairstreak, Satyr Anglewing
Dipper or Water Ouzel, Yellow-breasted Chat, Belted Kingfisher
Dusky-footed Woodrat

⤙

on the eve of that dark / bright shelf me
my name   licked my throat
with dust

      of herself's shelves
      put a few jelly jars there
      what colors what
      sin or sorrow what butter
      big butt & hilarious
      laughter, bright
      sifting powder to be
      seen in each

wind tunnel   water tunnel   tunnel of branches, leaves, and sky

In my topophiliac state
I am receiving & transmitting
international influence now—
    forget my sclerophyllic this
or that—
    bzz bzz tap tap

This place exists in how it compares to Kentucky,
Khartoum—that's its outside state
In the inside state, I was walking
up the mountain, on my way to Seven Falls
    when a naked man in a motorcycle helmet
    came running toward me

    Hey, girl!

    (Girl running on beach)
    (Girl worrying about fat legs)

Readers, predestined victims, now listen
    to all there is to say about anything, including
local anatomy,
    autonomy of all opossums, opossum anomie

    o, o, o opossum
    oh, reader

let this be to you

like sweet pao on Sunday
when the caracals come down from the mountain
& lick our ears
& the caged orang-utan busts free
like a golden-assed goddess *ex machina*
waiting for the tender life of
fur-lined avenues of trees
and I will
speak to thee succinctly
of March 4, 2003's dream:

"STRUM
STRUM"

I was a singer / harper, a poet
    to entertain the whores

I was 10 years old & a cunning
    little thief: I planned to
    rob the duchess / madame
    the house and all its customers
    in our seaside town by the sea

There were women with pearls & Chantilly
    ruffles, men in fedoras

        In a plot to
go on the open
road, I took the J-train downtown, steaming up the windows by french-
kissing strangers

I met my girlfriend on a hillside
She was an assistant to the duchess in this new boomtown
We made out on the dandelion hill; we entered the castle, I strategized

Here comes the duchess, a
raven-haired middle-aged cruel beauty
with new tennis shoes. I hide in her room, a room of latches

& stairwells & thick layers
of shining, cream-colored paint,
chiffon, organza, necklaces, no books of poetry
I hold as still as possible
but she comes into her closet-suites
& finds me standing there. She is surly
as a mad possum for
two seconds (I count them) then shows me
her new shoes—black side lace-up leather fancy
"tennis shoes"—& three brown
puppies on a leash at her
feet, which I pet; & my girlfriend
is whispering, "Did you see that, did you
see how she took to you? I've never seen her take
to anyone like that." I
say I know, It's the power of
the poet /
the harper / the singer who
casts some magic over
her ears & eyes

"STRUM
      STRUM"

Don't move s/he said, Your mood is resting
ever so on my sunlight & my sunset
is resting ever so delicately on that flattened
candelabra the SEA[viii]

No opossum is opposed to one p,
because they have opposable thumbs nor
to being the only marsupial marquisa on the continent,
philandering opossum of unfraudulent
thighs &
hanging from trees, toes
visibly seen. Visibly seen? What tautology, white
beast, you little
Algonquin, glowing in the
gutter in my dream

By my autumnal trees of opuscule all
pouches have been stopped and searched in the pitch-
black night amidst minor works of nature

Cops stuff meaty hands not delicate pawishnesses that leave tracks like the writing of eyelashes
but beefy & crammed into pockets searching for cocaine

Just so, La Migra stops opossums at borders with
  billy clubs, & sends them back
    whence they came   whence they came (c. 1906)[1]
      from South or East, stoned marsupials
        sipping on the golden soups of CA
          marble-eyed in the night & hanging, where
            do you lay your head, opossumness,

1 "Mr. J. R. Kocher, a jeweler who lived at Tenth and San Antonio streets, San Jose, imported, about 1910, seven opossums from Jackson County, Tennessee. At least five of the animals in this lot were known to have escaped from cages in San Jose. Other captive animals in this vicinity were thought to have escaped about the same time."

where do you play
on your optophones, converting light into sound & so
enabling the blind:
read this by ear

A man may know by heart the two hundred Spanish name-colors of horses,
and yet be easily tumbled off by any old brood mare.

—Antonio de Fierro Blanco[ix]

sine & cosine & radian argument
non-knowledge engulfs me

In the trackless desert   will I see
    a pillar of light[x]
burning tumbleweed blowing across the Great
Basin; "plainly men lived here, women
            died thereabouts"

I think it's too late
to make this poem
into a specific traffic (pall
of bright melancholy)

to know where I falls
on the inside or outside of time/space

too late   —   the marked
body
of the land has

submitted its own
dream & question

    seize me a city from that pale corridor, the future, traveling headfirst

        into the magnetized sun's dizzying pits

Instructions: Write the character's death scene, character
California, what would Character California
consider, what
egret flown from
the lake, what regret?

Plank Road, Highway 80, El Camino del Diablo
Jornada de la Muerte

the
California laurel is eaten raw or roasted with clover

Caligula has never been there O make this
mule give me counsel: shall we put
nuclear waste into unlined pits? *seek*
seeds of flame hidden
in veins of flint?

cloud-cover over the gold-diggers' ditch

makes it hard to think
& to think of time, its "ornamental
sleeplessness"

What will settle into sandstone, what soft event
be lost?[xi] Double the past from the present, cast it
out forward. Turn soft tissue to bone (writing)

5/25
The day opened cold, raw and windy
                   At night   blue-pill and oil   At evening   the wind went down
Distance, fourteen miles

5/30
Distance, nothing

5/31
Groups of men, inquiring
of lost cattle

         a kind of *terra firma* shipwreck
buffaloes   in considerable numbers

6/3
We were compelled to throw away
a quantity of iron, steel, trunks, valises, old clothes
and books . . . ; and I may observe here that we subsequently found the road lined with cast-off articles, piles of
bacon, flour, wagons, groceries, clothing

                             —Alonso Delano, *Across the Plains and Among the Diggings*

[July 17] —
A Diving bell and all the apparatus, heavy anvils
iron and steel, forges, bellows, lead, &c. &c. and provissions [sic];—

bacon in great piles, many chords of it—good meat. Bags of beans,
salt, &c. &c. Trunks, chests, tools of every description, clothing
tents, tent-poles, harness, &c. &c. . . . . . . [xii]

Discarded effects generally rendered useless:—Camp utensils & vessels broken
kegs & buckets stove, trunks chopped with hatchets, & saws & other
tools all broken. A considerable accumulation of ox-chains
& yokes . . .

[Oct. 20] —

Report of rifles, in the adjacent hills, answered by people here, —hunters, lost. . . .

—J. Goldsborough Bruff, *Gold Rush: The Journals, Drawings, and Other*
Papers of J. Goldsborough Bruff

In my seekness I
    salutate California as Empire
    which rendered us capsized
            to sizes of hipses & thighses

but like a burger I will rise
                in bits of bodily heat such as
god's abstinence to show
    the Sun's always a virgin in this assembled

paradise and every gray whale is gorging
    on amphipods amidst the quantum foam

Timetable

12,500 YEARS AGO	The Channel Islands are settled, "fire-reddened earth"; "glaciers tie up earth's water" (thus the islands were closer to shore)
10,000 YEARS AGO	Dwarf mammoth go extinct (overhunting?), "teeth found charred by fire"
8,000 YEARS AGO	*metates* & *manos* (milling slabs & hand stones)
2,000 YEARS AGO	Near present-day Santa Barbara arise large coastal villages; *syuhtun / syukhtun / ciucut,* province capital ($\approx$ 800 inhabitants); in that city, the Brotherhood-of-the-Canoe builds island-faring ships
1,700 YEARS AGO	Begin ball games, shell bead dollars, seawater warming; begin intermittent periods of severe drought; recent studies suggest the oceans were fished out; arrowheads dug into human bones
458	In Chinese records: the traveler Hui Shan makes note of a land with "tall trees"
1510	The first mention, in Montalvo's romance, of "California," an island "peopled by black women . . . who lived in the fashion of Amazons," a mythical place known for its wealth and gold
1524	Cortés to the King of Spain: "They tell me Ciguatan is an island inhabited by women. . . . They also tell me it is very rich in pearls and gold"
1540	Hernando de Alarcón enters at the mouth of the Gulf, touches California soil, sails 100 miles up the Colorado
1542	Juan Rodríguez Cabrillo[xiii] sails through: first documented contact between Chumash and Europeans; an estimated 100-120 languages spoken in what will come to be called California (*adel'tsuhdlv* in Cherokee, "where they find money"); an estimated 20-30,000 speakers of Chumash languages

1579	Francis Drake like a crowned pigeon took two small steps toward ships to softly plunder; from the top of a tree, saw; said, I'll sail an English ship in them seas. 1579: Drake's *Golden Hind*, loaded with circa twenty-six tons of repossessed silver, touches down on a lovely sliver of CA
1602	*Passing between the first [island] and the mainland, a canoe came out to us with two Indian fishermen, who had a great quantity of fish, rowing so swiftly that they seemed to fly. They came alongside without saying a word to us and went twice around us with so great a speed that it seemed impossible; this finished, they came aft, bowing their heads in the way of courtesy . . . After they had gone five Indians came in another canoe, so well-constructed and built that since Noah's ark a finer and lighter vessel with timbers better made has not been seen. (from The Diary of Sebastian Viscaíno, 1602-1603)*
1849	State constitution declares slavery illegal, but courts do not allow testimony from anyone not white. Blacks mine for gold to buy freedom ($1000)
1868	Federal "Peace Commission": "Schools should be established, which children should be required to attend; their barbarous dialects should be blotted out and the English language substituted"
1965	Mary Yee, last fluent speaker of Chumash, dies[xiv]
1967	Santa Barbara Song Sparrow goes extinct
CURRENTLY	Vandenberg Air Force Base plans to enlarge its facilities to construct a rocket-launching spaceport at Pt. Concepción (one of the oldest non-Native place-names in the U.S.), Chumash name *humqaq*—strategic as the gates from which the souls of the dead depart

In this nocturnal cosmorama, these
pictures and scenes from all over the land arrive & unfold

Suddenly, this atmosphere lends itself
to strange forms,   bizarre musics,   of the uncoverers

of early, earthly California;   A ship moves down
        Cape Flattery.   Was it an island, ruled by
Amazons, black, "to the right of the Indies"?

Do my eyes

                own this? Oh yes
                I think they do
                I spin them left
                I spin them right
                a cool geometry

Take me
down to swoon at large

among the jangling noises; clamoring tongues, yield up
your conquered plains; with a wagon and a bicycle I will take
California and all its free-
way lanes   with fear and favor over

my sweating edge of the sea

(An earthly beauty shines
through the broken lights)

(Dream called Nerve Lake)

(I was a child making up a child's songs,
singing to the Pebbles & Peerless Lachrymara, women
of great bitterness & sorrow who carry the history
of earth in a
starless sky)

A vast dark viscous lake
that divides cities at night
(leaping from)
rock to rock, umbrella
top to umbrella top, floating
milk carton to cigarette
box; there are bright
lights strung out on
edges of islands
but no way of telling which
[is your
looked-for]—because this lake
(of night) is so dense
—with refuse—
it holds a human's
weight on its trash—if you miss
you must struggle through
thick, black water to get
home—[where?]
[where is your looked-for?]

reprisal:

I was a waitress in a white dress,
an avocado goddess in the land of Phocis
Queen of the Drought in the kingdom
       of Prop. 13
I set forth
It was four blocks to the beach
What did I see there?
   a kegger with lots of young men
       preparing to drink[xv]

In the river Is, with bitumen,
near the town of that same name,
after the orders of turtles
snakes and lizards
twenty-six thousand two-hundred fifty days later, with intercalary months
when the reptiles finally gave up waters
& soft-shelled eggs,
past the baboon roosters of Egypt
one
representative of this
species arrived

After dark, it progressed through an elaborate
& perilous journey:
the soft separate hours of the night. Hello, Caesar, the Sun. The flesh of the gods was
gold and their bones were silver. Eleni was
5 foot 9.

Eleni, I
does not kill as readily
as other animals

"to abstract from my one self love, to enter it
in generality"

like all the relaxed hoplites
of Lydia, Eleni, float
out over the East
River

Float over, over,
over and out.

Eleni, Eleni (twinned)
w/ 2 legs / hearts.

of public
assistance, cleaned shit
out of state hospital pans; Herodotus thought
it strange miss eleni s elenying, intercepted report
cards mid-
mail yet graduated nevertheless. Nevertheless &
of such changes to the G, the E
the R. Such are trains. Oceans,
the amaze of paychecks, wheels & speech goddammit.
Make this easy to do that.
Make this easy to be that.
Make this easy to be that idealized form of American
beach bunnies

pretending to watch your boyfriend surf
or following his bliss on the beach with
a sixpack & roasted lizards
all the beach kids doing 360s off the lip

Come all ye Visigoths of Alaric
Huns of Attila, of the
Ostrogoths & Lombards, of hummingbird
& tigrillo   build a new Venice
over San Francisco where the
margin / marsh used to be

build me
hummingbird-sucks-it flower house over *syukhtun*

if no wood, build the house
with whale bone

poppy, says lizard, like the
sun itself
lying
on the ground
                if you are the clan   *of the traffic*
                if you are the clan   *of the hubcap*
                clan   *of carburetor*
                                          & reflective strips in the road

who
will your helper
be? what power, what plant
animal, vegetable, rock, what skunk dance

Offer the earth
money, what
will it
give you?

a   blue whale's chevron bones
the   hyoid to support the tongue
                               sycamore leaf-down, bound
                                         with
                                  spiderweb, Calliope's
                                         nested head)
my pelican skin robe, my
whale bone mortars, my   abalone fish hook
my   seal bone guessing game
my   aphid sugar
my   sea lion whiskers for drill bits
my   fattened bear cub for meat
my   "society ushered in with a happy rustle of bridal gowns and bank notes"

and the beauty of parking garages illuminated
in the night

⟨

a map immobilized the landscape
as if space were
a readable object

a lady just asked, why are all the cows
in California? All she saw from L.A. to Alhambra
were cows. In the Camargue, in France, in the Rhone delta was
once a sterile marshland but is now all about cow
Like one big intense cattle ranch, the
California is the Texas and the Riverside of Southern France

Paravent:

     in the folding of sheep, the penning
     of cattle, laying down
     of oysters, the parking of cars

     in the creasing of lambs, the origami
     of calves, the wrappling of grass

     in the pleating of the immortal soul
     of the automobile, the deadly knowledge in anthrax or
     minute radiating eruditions of anthracite, the tucking in
     of pinwheels, uranium enfolding at the anima of
     elemental centers, in the plaiting of the city of
     palm trees, the gathering up
     of glittering Venice Beach, in the fabulous history of *vaqueras,* the bending
     of wondrous fenders, in the folding membranes
     of organelles, organized & specialized to make me believe
     in the plastering of castor plants, & unsurpassable statues of cows

Now how shall it

recalcitrate upon its approved
forms and quit them? How shall the droning world get on
without all its *beaux esprits* in California? Each harbors its own menagerie
of mesozoan parasites. Each to each may I personally undress
the periosteal filaments
of California, & all its
stockinets?

No, you may not.

Let birds of delivery bearing drugs of
        wonder & weather show me
                a providential acquaintance with men & women
                        who can wheel it better on the wing than me, who can hoof it
                        far past the surplus of stars in deed or in thought, dead-of-night & niggardly

Let Leviathans in the land of Beavers take refuge in the ark of daylight

But let E. kiss with the rabbit the dew-struck grass
in the morning, sun-
        light slapping her face

Let E., foster parent of a sparrow praise without end the porcupine, which is a creature who once bristled in my pan
Let Br'er Rabbit bless with the oleander and his people the pillbug, a living mineral & silver

roundhouse rolling

       beneath the leaf

Red-tailed kite blessed be ELENI & her friends in falcons & in the MALL, stealing transistor radios from Robinsons
    at San Roque

Let the possum beg god for his wily fame, inaccessible

Let me praise with the flea his sharpened tongue, leap up from the carpet, my bitter biting friend

Let E. bless the barn owl of gravity amongst my guests

When you consider the gulliest of birds, remember one-thousand and one nights of *Laridae*—jaegers,
       gulls, skimmers, & terns free and far from Laredo, generalist feeders, scavengers, sometime
       saprophytes, skimming on flesh living and dead; Yet let you sing, Caspian Tern,
       silver above,
       white below:—*kra haa*
       Sterna elegans—*car-eek*
       Sterna hirundo—*kee-arr*
       Sterna forsteri—*kay-r-r-r, kip kip kip*

Glaucous-winged gull, screeching *kow-kow-kow,* soft-toned *ga-ga,* let the partygoers go
       in the grass and fuck in the night

Let the power of Coney Island come to this place, with its wonderwheel and frightened midnight grit

Let burning glass illuminate the power of darkness

Eleni be gracious to the windows indeed lest they show me how strangers are grubbing up my
                                     manzanita trees

Let E., me, keep yapping, "for EARTH is an intelligence" in all her vestments & pants

Let California awake us from our dressed-up stupor
    by which I don't get shit done

"For the names & the numbers of animals are as the names & numbers of stars"
    & they are distracting me

whale bones

Where are we?
Bad Water.
What city are we in?
In tinder-dry CA
When the French came, they called it
      Les Anges, but before that we called it
Los Angeles de los Stinking Devils *(diables puants), Bahia de los Fumos*

      hear
      the ricotta recitation of words
      in a vast, languageless land

      what I velcroed myself out of:
      a spinning rip through lawless language

what eroded buffer between
civilization, ferity?

      I cannot catalogue
      all the false histories
      that wobbled through

      I'm getting too much distortion

& feedback out of the speaker—
mythologizing the landscape beyond recognition
like some simulacra of *Saturday Night Fever*
with a touch of the East
These coastal mountain ranges may low like
cattle in love, but

Writer, make us a sea we can believe in

flesh corrupting below waves
going down hard & coming up soft

     That's better

& they are so branch-boundlessly human
that I did not learn kind words
     between men & women

till "the soggy clods became lovers & lamps" burning in night-fields

my grandmother's mynah bird
escapes its small cage, flits
through irrigated groves south of Tehachapi, over oasis-
laden fire-riddled deserts, with a wing for
     "fly, happiness
     stay, happiness"   Rise up

In the cold-crusted East
catch a swarm of blackbirds stenographing the sky

[Make promises to birds[xvi]]

Sky a moving wave made of wings & they did not
stop, or want to stop, pouring between buildings in chafing braille

Can you
read that wingy language? Can you
typeset that sky? Rewrite this
strange vast present and past

to refute Descartes' ideas
of what has always been found in me in sleep?

all that entered into the composition of the bone or the stone that smashed it
was more perfect than me

Me, making out with some hoofed mammals up north (pronghorn antelope), kissing
a long-tailed weasel

No luxuries I knew but
worm-eater, herbivore,

winter astrostratus
ragged-up cap-clouds or saucer-shaped lenticulars (savory
fried up with dill & butter)

Habitat corridors for jackrabbit movements in & out without a velvet boxed yellow desert
Smoketrees off to the south in the rain shadow

This mathematical expression of light
is not light
It is merely a suggestion
of what light might be

as all the myth & knowledge any
place carries with it is imparted to the child—

      foxtail spikes may catch
      in a dog's nose or eyes

      if you get lost in the woods
      eat miner's lettuce

      ghost shrimp cannot haunt you, child

What about the boy dragged down by a puma at Gaviota?
    Whose home was he in, girl?

        a nest of bowering threads feeding on Jewelweed, the parasite "Love-
    vine" that twines[xvii]
to kiss you
by the barley   blue-green   in sunlight

fool in sunlight
meditating on daily objects—
to find any aura & possible identity

signees & signets
a sideslip, a skid, a
downward turn toward the inside
temblor

oak as a   sign-tree
              split-tree
              spit-tree

the god of imaginable objects
made me

or

Something you didn't notice accruing, like light
pollution, & when you
tried to see the stars, they were gone

See the world
mathematically?
wave's curves
or curl of thirstling sound

Draw the world from memory

No, that's a banana
Now practice
practice your curves—
Practice drawing
it, this
world

curve of horizon

eucalyptus pod

jagged rag of torn breaker

peeling in in threads of
white appetite
for wreckage

When it "breaks," we can say it "shatters,"
but there is   behind   the breaking line the
                                            blind horizon line
and no thing will be broken again
        till another shore (miles and miles past rough sea)

        border curve — world's curve — his voice curving past — a

            baseball — its — bat — bat — wings — arcing toward — dark — euca-
                                                    lyptus leaf — what

        lopsided, what symmetry

"What chemistry!
That the winds are not really infectious,
That this is no cheat, this transparent green-wash of the sea which is so amorous after me,
That it is safe to allow it to lick my naked body all over with its tongues"

California
gives sqwooshy kisses one by one

the liquid shimmer over the sandpapery surface of the earth

above: hang gliders: huge ribonucleic rubber birds do not remember

the guy upon whom the beach cliff
fell—one minute he was sitting innocently
in the sun on the evil beach
the next his bones were a pile of
jelly & the sack was the skin
& he was crushed, & he died

The rough & tumble D.P.[2] guys like a good-bad god squad; if you dance
        they'll break your face

They know nothing
        of the appeal of miniaturized space

Back at the Jurassic (smogging out the Channel Islands in a dun-colored haze) oil
in the air, the hair
of birds, "brillo birds," hello
to my mother's nostalgia for Haight / Ashbury like a tailless dog loping

2 Dos Pueblos High School, Goleta, built on or near the site of *mikiw,* two Chumash villages.

through parks and owners with plastic bags tied on for shoes

In California, they like to stand around and pant a lot

I'll go fell three grumpy bears

Feed me
my archaic needs nights, no truck with

the mysterious curve
of the earth
pulling in
to the golden cities

and the waves flattened & the waves rise up & increase
their drag & the shore receives them: wave and wave and wave and wave
"And so on and on to the shore . . . if you think from the sea
and if you think from the shore, it
touches and breaks." Torsion
in the first Möbius strip cannot compete with the waves' amoebic figure 8
and as the course projects happily hypothetically straight from the wave and around
the world mathematically, perfectly ragged   the unified field of wave
and wave & water & pull   creature / tide
work out that ideal
the drift of it everything

Wherever shallow, standing water remains; along the coast in brackish loops, around springs, ponds, lakes, and sluggish streams.

> *Common Tule, Bulrush, Cattails, sedge and spike rush, pondweed*
> *Predaceous diving beetle, Giant Water Bug, toadbug*
> *Gallinule, Coot, Marsh Wren, Redwinged Blackbird, Yellowthroat*
> *Pond turtles, Treefrogs, Garter snakes*

I believe I said

in secret chambers
of the human
heart
in
Gold Ruin
amongst hydraulic quark scars
walked Dante
through
tule fog
bunchgrass
yerba santa & chamise, chinquapin, in
tinder-dry CA
in deserts turned to great cities
there were "books . . . . . . in the . . . . . . brooks"
babbling great poetry

we coined the word
hoodlum for idle
men &
women who loitered
around sand-
lots
where unfold
the limbs of juvenile

delinquents straight
from the womb

evanescent gifts, the gold-spiked tips
by which we divide this
garden from that

amid squatter riots in Sacramento
        shootouts at Mussel Slough

California's polarization

into light &
dark   tight
& loose
sectors of
stars
stars
night

now empty California
of its patterns
of maximum
profit

in my little 2 ft. x 2 ft. plot
cleared
of thought

The Yucca, (or Spanish Dagger), with its beautiful panicle of waxen bells is a familiar sight in the foot hills of California. "God's Candle", as it was named by the early settlers grows from six to ten feet tall. Its fruit is utilized widely by the Indians and the unique wood is often used for novelties.

835

Dear Margaret: I am having a fine time and seeing so many interesting things. I hope everything is going well. Did I tell you Oliver sold

LOS ANGELES SEP 4 12:30 PM 1947 CALIF.

SAVE THE EASY WAY BUY U.S. BONDS ON PAYROLL SAVINGS

UNITED STATES

*Mrs. Burton Kramer
2200 Wadsworth
Denver 14,
Colorado.*

"You are mistaken," I replied.

. . .

"How mistaken?"

"Why," I answered, "you are not fighting for California."

"What the d——l then am I fighting for?"

—Edwin Bryant, *What I Saw in California*

dream: all the wild beaches had been built upon

Fancy hotels with eyeless, edgeless pools and all
rotting piers ripped out They built hundreds
of hotels a night on Haskells' wild shores for Tom Hanks's weekends

To the south, my beaches have been given over
to oil-
drilling companies, cargo
wharves, factory-built
blackness by the sea, squatting
buildings, black smoke
up to the edge of the water, concrete
haunches jumbled

and built blackness right into the water—
a huge city lurking in absence of light lies
under the waves
as they roll—roll *evil.*

I have found one patch left—lucent creatures drift
along the coral under a
clean sea—an electrically-purple Elegant
Nudibranch (*Flabellinopsis iodinea*) with neon orange
fringe, Hopkins' Rosy Nudibranch, red crabs, turning with the water in an
easy metropolis of sea—

but sooted lands lie at the Southern right, and I know
soon it will slip up in the night, with
the will of the people, & engulf this last bright
animal ditch.

In the dream I was hunting for dinner—razorback clams, any
soft-bodied animal that oozes at the edges
of symmetry, anything delicious, wearable,
lovely

Removing the heart of the turtle to a jar
of saltwater, it will beat when prodded twenty-
four hours later
the mermaid's purse is a sandshark unhatched & now the tiny fish is pickled in alcohol
a turtle's flesh will continue to respond even
when you place the white cubes of
meat
in a pot

moving pictures of the color & patterns
change in the bonito during death
as they beat their tails against the deck, colors pulse & fade, pulse & fade and then they are dead

animals have one color when they are alive
another when dead

      "This smooth blue water runs out of time, . . . and a kind of dream" sits in it

the "playing porpoises" do not "play opposites," "turtles, the great schools of fish" under
the ruffled waters
all the thing was alive and alive when
you saw it   the teeming surface of the watery
earth   barnacle & hydroid riding the turtle's
back   pelagic rock-lobsters in his gut   a crab
inhabits his ass   the waters stuffed

with living plankton through which the big fish
swim

moving pictures of langostino littering
the water's currents & soon put them in a white porcelain pan

now the film is
"immersed . . . in alcohol which promptly removed
their brilliant color"

"the heat of a great furnace" (Cortés), *Calida fornax*
not the denomination of New Mexico, Apaches' land
but of shorespeople, *sxa'min,* a small sea cave and arch, sexy *cala-y-fornix,* rooted
in primitive magics, names
will stick or fall away, a list

of disappearances

what disappeared, has
disappeared, is
disappearing, will disappear. I can't tell for they are
disappearing. It is happening
around us in forests, on highways. What
is appearing? This remains to be
named and seen.

With soft foots & mean teeth
bite I mean
bite Holyfield's ear
twice
between the world
destroyed & the world
restored walk blithe
                    smooth   gay
yield up fame & flame

                        in a house of dust / persimmons, native
                              home to Chicken Little, Please do remember Chicken Little
and the sky
must fall in pieces of blue
all over this place

all my sweaters stolen
all my things lost & stolen
in the dark dream of that state, fish
nibbling at the coast in
blackened water, coastline
eroding into sea, my
sweaters whisked away by
ecstatic thieves   across cliffs, into
rich houses tucked into folds
between hills   in my hometown I can't
afford to live in; all my houses,
rooms, apartments, bicycles, cars,
anything I could
never afford to own stolen
from me in California
& silver earrings' backs, parts
of earrings
crumbling into backseats
as we drive up
the coast in California, California

corroding country of such crumbling

& that country
is speaking a guiltless language in my dream

to show me something
I don't understand, e.g.,

                                    seconds will
                                      conceive
                             of this city or space
                         as a blind person does—
piles of   rock   rubble   dirt thrown up   each yard, lot
                           each spatial block
                    of heat and chill and shape
                         without color[3]

                     "This is how hours stand still"

3 except *amarillo*

In the dream of cities I've seen I've seen that city before

walking up to the grocery store in the dark for laundry quarters & ice
cream   a city
unknown & mystery like
when I had never seen cities before

      The supermarket aisles are empty but
      at the checkout line huddle masses

I have a lover with dark hair, he is my other, he is
as they say, good to me   We eat rice
at a minute-wine bar (small ceramic tumblers with
two chambers curved as
tulip vaults litter the table—they are for a minute's
worth of wine, for a minute is all you have
left to live or drink)   Whistler rockets fly in the night like streak-assed fire-
      flies that bear destruction

My love & I, as we always do
we do lie down

Spirits have been here & \ there around us—

Wait, my lover says, if you want to see angels you have to see
the OTHER angels   We drive
through an Xed-out part of town   brick buildings four stories up

& everywhere wicked angels are floating—out of
windows & off rooftops
glowing harbors of light
where eyes should be   Ah, so it's
not all easy in the life of an angel
You really *can* become a bad-
ass cherub, & we float up & up
around a column of ice till
at the top we too my love and I
are angels half-buried in a snowbank
that keeps things frozen down below
so that no people can move
as they'd really like to move
arms or hands or hearts
Because we all know
if you cannot be
a bad angel, there is no other angel to be; now we too
can be naked & sleeping, our bodies wrapped
round each other, backbones showing, buried
in ice & snow, & so

     the world goes on around us, harboring night-hunters

        any oxygen void
        any air raid
        any siren
        any bright tracer
        any signs or suns or guns in true dark sky
        any humbling night
        any hunting
        any animal haunches slipping
            rippling muscle in desert sand

any palette in shreds
any false gift of food
any bed on your floor
any neighbor, any adult or child
any rocky outcrop
any rabbit destroyed
any arm or horse prepared for war
any piece of earth or dirt
any women, any men, bless them, for they have
                    all gone out of their minds

Nobody will die in love or rise
            to give the tired rider their place
Nobody will keep their feet off the seats

There will be no F train, no voice-over over the intercom, no
                    place to go
                    more worthy than this interior surface
                            of hyper nerves in the jangling consequence /
                            inconsequence of *things*

California,

I would like to say:

I accept this destruction
this consolidation of ardent clouds
but instead, I write:

California,

Bring back Karl Malden & oral sex sweaty and scratched under tennis-court bushes by daylight
before they sent my Led Zeppelin records skidding across Old Coast Highway
Bring back my bibliomancy when John Steinbeck said,

> "If it comes onto rain—why
> a little rain don't hurt a horse."

and bezoar stones in cows'
stomachs to cure fat thighs

wind-brought gall wasps
making moss on roses

Bring back Walt Whitman in the bathroom

this horse and *that tree*

me, born for action

Bring back our Beaufort scale, spinning
winds to speed us from
obscurity to glory,
bingeing on Herodotus

Bright spores of daylight,
Belle de Nature, come see

4 x 4 destruction:
memory
history
cities
me

magnetic levitation of the rush orange, loquat trees
        flying toward the sun

        I crawl & spit
            unsolvable pits, two slick stones arguing under the tongue *(Eriobotrya japonica, famille de rose)*

In my magesterium, teach trees that I am a vector with magnificent gestures
        with mansuetude, *ma non troppo*

Tree, a harbored thought in seed,
        creep into the boughs with me
        & my uncount noun, happiness

        when the mynah bird escapes its cage give a wing for

            a slow happiness a sad happiness a shy
            or sly a
            fly, happiness

wrap my tongue around the slug / (past flesh) mantillad fruit
this magic bullet-seed

            is for another life; to shoot us out past smash

loquats are three for a quarter at my sidewalk stand; stones
are five for a dollar

Orange Interlude
+ one Short Sea

My mouth
opened wide & out
came the world howl
They cut
the umbilical too far
from the heart, a
stump—this
was the marvel, the navel
California came out of, round
& warm as an orange
lament on a trembling
tongue

⤙

In the belly of the lily live
erupting ochre
bead heads—mini-
scule orangestation twisted
into a tree, lobes disguised
as pollen lamps

at dusk, a flickering: on-off-on-off

⤙

a man who has
lived in
hazardous
lizardous
light, a highway
cone smelted
into round
gold that shows
us the slackened
road at night, with
the grace of an
orange, one can
run
over water
without ever
sinking (some ancient
men & women
learned that)

⊰

primavera
substance, fertility
drug, Dymaxion blossoms
under the orange
hand, from jewel-crusted dirt
the fringe a skirt

Annabergite leaves
Antlerite   Labradorite   Sodalite
olivine   cabrerite   Torbernite leaves
unrigging in
the breeze

This orange wears
no fustanella!
This orange tree is naked!
as the inside of veins

⨽

ravenous, blackly
circling a
girdled roadblocked circular lock
box ho! buck-
minster fuller
geodesic
dome
house—we can replace
the garden's roof
tiles—you
mirage—shimmer
of sweated water
across
tarmac

⨽

Carpinteria is fisting it out
with Florida but the oranges of Santa Clara are
all over

⨽

Here is the

big blue composition where we see
the sea in its big blue
bleeding green hat
its big blue bleeding blue
     cape
where we see the sea in its big blue
bleeding white spittle cap
  big blue bleeding   whale body sea
as painted by Nicolas de Stael from
an aerial view   just this much—
one big square cadre-of-the-never-
ending big blue bleeding green
sea [flat heaven]

"eased with thoughts of sun or rain"

I went down to the crystal South
in a sack of flesh
locking onto guide stars,
                              drinking up
available starlight

August: my reptilian brain says
Go to Coney Island
to get your head
        closer to the ground

September, misfortune rolled us back
from wonderwheels heeled in sand

November, the waterspouts dancing devils on the far horizon of aqua
to be wrestled with for the world's "more solid prizes, the ceaseless
                                        vehicles of tide"

I too will wrestle with the human hurricane, hulking black storm

        —Wait, what is
        "the human"?   :   the will, & "I have a hand"
        that disintegrates into darkness

        fate, false history, I cannot
        make this list because
        another it

is "at it with a vengeance, and what [this]
it is is Nature"

the biomedical engineering labs of soft cnidaria
Till the gastropods & Pismo
clam can pull the plug on
public sources of power

the crystalline style of
amylase found in the
White Venus clam's belly
will rise and write:

"any peasant with a dumb
cow can make whipped
cream but it takes a chemical factory
in California to make Cool Whip"

Passing on to a planetary and electronic
hotplate . . . as animal organs are orphaned / replaced
by my motherboard lattices in the new
articulation of civic space

The crystalline style
will rise and write:

"not an animal gives a hip-
hop, the moon
is made of cold rice
it will drop you a clump
if you're good people
on earth"

If a body
fell or if I did

through a hole in the bottom of the sea-

floor—a door—then I
could say that I was swimming

through the shadow of water to invent a language, dark engine
to cut down address

Soon, a swallowtail occurred in that dialect
        a hummingbird-as-camera, bright Alexander
              discovered a leaf   a tree grew   several
          islands, an ocean   I made

birthmarks at the napes of the necks, the wet
recesses of backroads, marshlands,
glasses of water sweating and
drowning children on beaches where fog collects

to drown all you countrywomen
and drown you my
countrymen

and our speeches that drown
out the sound of the Ocean Sea

as any sea dreams
of being a hole through which to slip
a rhetoric above cognitive sound

Here is a glass of water to be drunk
by the things
things dream of or think

I think that's mean ("drown you"), but I dreamed a softer thing: I dreamed

      that dust mote was the first word ever I wrote
      when I first wrote it would be something
      to be floating in beams of light, very
      tiny, nightly,
                lightly

[*porchlight's halo surrounded by evening; not a sound*]

so slide this one into the stereoscope and see
how it measures up—O.K.
O.K. I will as soon as we are not
ourselves gifted

with a worldly soul, I will
not receive my life but
from others or I will
be durable / drunk with tenderness
for the surfer, lizard

I need only a little boat to discover / deliver
my liver, Fort Spiritual, beached on Haskells grit

in the dream
of a landscape dream in which
I am not, a parallax practice
to crumbling More Mesa cliffs

my ideal dream of a landscape dream in which
I am not, a false utopia. "A shadow is a door to walk through" because of the vistas, pit-
falls and snares; this sea is a seventh helix
higher than the rest, with names

of pirates still scratched into the rock (that's history); abandon
the pinnace, the coast-gun; stud the point

with curling monsters; but to this beach will
beautiful women come?

    In sun-helmets come down to the beach, J.S. continued, the intrepid
interloping cormorants in radical black diving subversively
off cliffs to catch the fishermen's fish
"And they are . . . slaughtered, as all radicals should be," *Heliaster kubiniji*

dark pendant gorgonians swaying under reefs

The urchin diver brought me back many tiny abalone like fetus ears and thimbles   each week
                                                                    pounding
                                                the meat; we kissed
                                under sheets
                                        of water;

For my pelagic perfect cosine wave
that holothurian travel game

there may be dust on that border between South and Central
but the dividing line between land and sea is no line at all
Mussel homesteads on pier pilings, colonial castles of worms
Each limpet's got a personal grazing ground of brightly-lit sea lettuce it keeps new-mown neat

Hermaphroditic sea-hares slime around
                                a Troglodytic Chiton perambulates in elliptical
                                                                        pits   Sea-
            cradles rasp off lichen in rough minor-chordal ancient armor, and Darwin's
"in a bos'n's chair slung over the side of the boat scooping up jelly-fish" in his fist

Starfish in the brittle numb curricula
      make secondary pentamerous radial symmetry[xviii] / radical syllabi; the Asterozoa might teach us
         autotomous habits, how
         to grow back an arm
      Fiddlers bubble, Sally Lightfoots clack over rocks
   Tegula funebralis (Turban Snail) is wrapped & folding (spine worn away), feeding (on soft weeds)

And when they're done one hundred seventy tons of crashing water come

An eighty-ton rock moved 70 ghosty feet across the beach

     How to hide
         from fluid muscled wreckingball fists? Some clams
            never emerge from sand.

At Monterey, I collected 136 hermit crabs to uncover the mysteries of population dynamics. Who is the hermit crab's enemy? How do they make their cities? Conquistador, invader, a hermit crab builds municipalities in mudflats: it looks like nothing but crab castles of ready-made mud and shells and rocks. An animal's *Bildungsroman*, a neospiritual discovery of what cannot be built from scratch

"The killing and relaxing and preserving took us until dark, and even after dark we sat and made the labels to go into the tubes." A person builds a collection (tabulating animals), tearing off pieces of species. But a chiton has a girdle! teeth of magnetite they make themselves! a Jackfrost Moss crochets a lacy pattern on rock and retires to its "little limy coffin-shaped" quarters . . .

"This bottle, this glass, a big stone on the deserted beach—these are immobile things, but they unleash a tremendous movement in my mind. I do not feel that when I see a human being moving around like an idiot. . . . Immobility makes me think of vast spaces that contain
movements that do not stop, movements that have no end."   (Joan Miro)

"12-month flowers experienced," and tectibranchs and bryozoa, and down to the Mexican sea
Here is what has come to surface after so many
convulsions:
"The flame of materials"
amaze

⤙

Suddenly, everything belongs in California,
the "sodium squalls," tomatoes
of injustice, Hatshepsut's columns, Sweetheart,
you, and drinking straws.

      "And I will show you
that whatever happens to anybody can be turned to beautiful results," like Junipero Serra
& his slaves building missions, "these twenty-one precious jewels" that grace our coast

in the land of neophyte beasts, rats in the palms
      They raised a few oranges, made soap, some iron & leather
           Serra accumulated . . . torn flesh, *pinche cabrón* his breath . . .

              a tablecloth of dark cloud, black dust sifting down

The sun is hot & meanly
burning golden welding holes in the sky
Close your eyes in the April green of elms, Robert
      Browning, to be in your poems or for you to be here in this one

that sails to annex
      all tangled bluffs, restless eagles' angles, "to confront night, storms, ridicule, accidents,
           rebuffs, as the animals and trees do"

California in the afternoon of later California, singing insects with stinging hearts, the bland

atmosphere of Santa Barbara land, hometowns invaded by Huguenots, Reaganites
Daughters of the Did you wait for our languages to disappear?
Did you wait with an indicative hand on islands?

The Colorado is a tourist here, silver &
    braceleted, a collar

of rock like Serra's

the ghosts of Yokut braves floating up
in the mists from that very crooked stream, the San Joaquin

A California song,

A prophecy and indirection, a
thought impalpable to breathe as air

—WW

But this, but you—small, pitiful and twiggy—

—The *Odyssey*

According to my lights
as I circle & touch upon this state or that
uncouth gringos are lounging in the shade

harmonica-players in Grass Valley pull salmon out of chaotic rivers
real-life vampires who chew Bazooka only go out at night
and up in Humboldt someone's getting 10 bucks an hour to trim weed

I'd like to fit *you* into this
rectangle which was
the courthouse at Tehachapi   One can arrive
on a motorbike or walk there
by moonlight across oasised
deserts, through irrigated groves. I walked there in the
heat & in the night & by the moon I heard

the song my cat's ears made traveling
over tiny ridges in sand—Did you, Mr.
Stevens, sneaking through? When Odysseus
went to sleep, s/he did not

need a
book in the desert. She *was*
the book.

If a succoring arm would come buckle me
like a tenement, a heavy object attached to this bodily vessel
to stabilize reports running into nail-laden driftwood on Goleta's beaches
or teach me to speak

Hindi out of the blue
      The snoring wind wrapped

round the house tonight & banged the door
against my head you can't say "Music
comes from God," that's just silly my friends were
trying to explain me in the situation in the
future if it were to speak
it would speak of you:
When darkness was caming
what you write you can drop it
in the sea

RISE UP, ———— phonemes
cum genomes, let
language disintegrate, tiny
technology in the compost heap; gumdrops; I mean
our species; the ovicidal moonfish slips
into Sirius, Canis Major-bright my words, dive-
bombing swallows angry at my hair & slip
new gods

into the sky, the whites

of their eyes in the aerial
and orbital annals of the rotations of earth & moon, with reference
to the background of stars, I reposition
all bodily organs, effulgent
fruit fractioned into pistil parts
simpering on the vine; make this god
                                        a   mountainlionface
with a woman's lips, that one a   monster   boy   spread out   across
                the sky. And in the potato bugs' and earwigs'
myth of the rape
of tomatoes new things are birthed, new
constellations, new creatures, born;

in the frightened upper
atmosphere, appearing
in the hemisphere above us

in the most ecumenically
expensive country measured out in mean solar time
a flawed human body with golden, molten veins

       —Sugar, there comes a time

when a woman needs most
    water,   rain,   cloud,   rock, flower, dirt

       —Stranger, the sea

is a meadow of ripe saltwater aloft hiding treasures, surface tension
an inverse lens
magnifying
the Bathing
Place of my many-times-bright sardines

By adjunct grace do
        kelp blossoms surge
    in the race of the West

    from Earth. All rise.

A thought wavy and loose
showed me
the endings of matter, things
beyond
hope, gold cuffs of
long distances drawn on the jaw; as the chemical eye

adjusts, dark adaptation; there are places the light of thought
does not penetrate; reverberations in space.   There are songs too long to sing, i.e.,
the power to measure pebbles, e.g., all the
ones in that sea, so pigeons
pinioning, pioneers, let's us
swish out with the light.

On the summit
At the Hesperian end   In the vast
magnetic
saddles
of earth   was cradled
the Annapurna Everest Ocean Sea
sliding out all fences sliding back the standing
mountains, the big black lake in which I could not
feel safe, life; like

Great Whites with sexual claspers who must move & love all the time
would love my limbs but spit
out the flesh.[xix]   Slide back, sea, so we can see

the bright

bathing bathers of the big black lake, SPACE, bodies like golden
apples hanging on the dark branch, EARTH, like
Great Alexander or Eleni or little children finding the ripest apples, last places to be within;

kissing mystical ventral surfaces, occiscles; rise up
for arboreal views
            of passionate showy brittle stars *(Ophiuroidea)*, mirror of watery earth & sky;[xx]

Uncle Aristotle's lantern, urchin, my mouth remains close to the rock
while the shell falls

off; enter the

sun, such the masseur bully sun
big fiery fruit in his rhymes of ray-on-stone, pounding
the flesh, the one, one, the one
sun was the
melancholy team sun in
matrices whose elements are birds
(words) whose elements are branches,
ladders, shadows, shadders, birds

Death Valley Automobile Trip, 1926

" The road at the entrance of 'Devil's golf course"

a physiography simple
a mountain fringe along the rim of ocean
a splendid valley of imperial extent
a great area of arid, barren land
a big block of the Earth's crust faulted & tilted into sharp
escarpment, a gentle curvy slope at its back, the finest mountains offerable
rising 10,000 miles above the sea

The tectonics of
props we
lay upon
proved themselves willing
to shift

I too, moving viewer
in the indeterminate land, an always-moving
horizon at my front
or at my back

The mere experience
of walking back
the way I came
changed everything
I saw: the come-alongs unhitched

Walking and looking into a landscape, I said
ah ha
can I change this?

      to bend
      to nudge
      to erode
      to tar
      to road

In the northern schema, mountain scenery of
granite pinnacles
amphitheaters of Tuolumne tumbling walls and towering rock
polished meadows and falling water make their own adjustment
to surfaces & death.

South of the fork
of the rushing King is where my friend Adam Davies went
down in the River's
torqued ellipses;

Therein lies my first *Museum*:

Lachrymae musarum

I'm sorry for the dead today in a dream
of Adam, a little scar on his accordion elbow, he was
playing for money on the Metro

He had grown big into his limbs as if he'd never slipped on the rock, not
drowned in a tunnel of leaves

In the dream he had the interior prestige
of being human & not

as opposed to animals but he was that
solid, simple I

loved him the way the living
tend toward the dead. In the Book
of Ease, we floated

cloths in the pond
till the insects' dust rose

& caught there
the wings of moths—

What is a pure number
without unit? A cloth

of skin with no stitches, no
other clothes

canyons the work of rivers, glaciers,
lakes, of meteors, craters
(What do they make at China Lake? Lapsarian. Lap-lap up the lake.)
Upon the plains north of the spiritual river
up from the Narrating Bay
reservations lie dusty and secretive in the muddy recesses of the map

What does the story say?

It says earlier inhabitants
gave this place Modoc Sisquoc Lompoc Cuyapaipe Ojai
Coachella Naciemento Siskiyou Tehama Tuolumne Hetch-Hetchy Tulare Sequoia Yosemite[xxi]

In California we have our own Idyllwild, Elsinore, Wildomar, Paiute, Badwater
Siquos, Los Coyotes I.R., May you rest in peace, Quartz Hill, Fawnskin City, where Blake
        stuck his finger into the bloody deer and all you ghosts who could give a fuck
                about aesthetics, that strictly human endeavor

Chocolate Mountains melting into the Salton Sea
Zzyzx, Devil's Postpile, Lone Pine
Terrabella, Hesperia, Johannesburg, in California
we have our own Johannesburg

Did we have pippesewa, that Cree ever-
green?

In *californium* (radioactive), we teach you   (*curium*)
calisthenics for *call-boys*
days of deep *calenture*   sailors in tropical delirium
imagine the sea to be   fields of wheat

                              (sea grown bitter with the salt
                              of continents)

Cities floated in enormous hot
  tubes / tubs of incandescent light

In the beginning

  cells discovered the magic
        of chlorophyll, in the days of our early
              symbiogenesis, redwoods like great "candelabra held blue green algae
              up to the light" & sponges branched
    toward the divisions in a spine   tunicate, tunicate   This is the tourist's version

    of fruiting weeds that sway with the tides   plucked from rock & cast adrift

        a frame-by   frame dream, state
              of gold-bottomed spinning

In the beginning, California thought

take off my gown of bruised spectacle (oscillation
        of liquid earth); see moon scars under the Pacific; take off my dress
                        (of impressed dissatisfaction) —
                a great wave is torn away & hurled to space

Night's dimensions blink & alternate
        with the palely flaming head of Lana Turner, to say
what movies

did to my past,   light-
harvesting viruses   splice
memory

                                the ghosts of beautiful
                                dead
                                actresses float
                                round bits of celluloid
                                to haunt their own scenes of rain & cars &
                                trees over & over[xxii] Is the land
                                laid out
                                like that? Our own private scenes of storms & oaks,
                                cars on night roads
                                haunted
                                haunted like that?

In the beginning our bodies cast their shadows across the screen, protoplasmic

before Monterey was "rosemary and sweet whiskey and whoopin' and yellin'"
and Brando, photovoltaic & glowering like a grubworm, uttered, "Get up, you big tub a guts"

Because the muds shook like jelly, and I thought
bathoearth, behemoth, can San Andreas scar
across the Carrizo plain
like a skidding dirtbike ripping up turf and
liquefying earth, a
sixty-mile mad necklace, bracelet at the splintered boundary of some dancer's wrist

silts & salt on stilts, Sierras our
                    "granite napkins folding & refolding
          in our laps"

This coastal calico, ocean-atticful of objects from around the Pacific world   California
is the palace where we're making continents up

          (sand, sand dollar, rock . . .) Your job is to

tell the history of each & every piece

Begin with lost houses
     lost loves
          lost boxes or keys

Continue with a description
    of a journey

Conclude with the real
    subject

        which is
            quiescence
            among the trees

        reflecting
        a way to extinguish the will

        a nurseling wind
            gone berserk

        through noctilucent clouds
            in high summer
                    high sky

            made soft & breezy, the wild
        wind having taken the piss
                out of it

        It, the sky, that is

Invent a language, "the tongue
of the mirror," into which
anything, everything can be
perfectly translated, but in which
nothing can be said

& from every train window you will see house-
lined streets radiating over the curved earth

Dense cover of evergreen shrubs with thick leathery leaves over plains, mesas, foothills; many with fire-resistant seeds that sprout quickly, and only, after fires.

> *Chamise, Scrub Oak, Hard Tack, wild lilac, Bear Brush & Quinine, manzanita, Sugarbush*
> *Mountain Quail & Scrub jay, Wrentit*
> *Bluebelly, Fence & Horned Lizards, Striped Racer, Rattlesnake*
> *Silk Moth, Hedge-Row Hairstreak, Callippe Fritillary, mariposa, mariposa, mariposa*
> *Mule Deer, Coyote, Gray Fox & Brush Rabbit, California Pocket Mouse, Nimble*
> *Kangaroo Rat, Chupacabras &*

Bobcats exploding with design, a symmetry for the mind
to take shape in

May we also be mentioned in quakes that shake us without regard to season or weather
Specific and spiritual tremors, atomically incorrect, nomenclaturally "extremely severe"

1812, Santa Rosa / *wi'ma*: "the waters receded from the island several hundred yards."[xxiii]
We are violently disturbed, 1906
Gin Chow placed a note in the Post
      Office: an earthquake will hit (1925)[xxiv]
and in '78, I had to run from the theater, from a country extremely rough. It went like this:

        Under fluorescent lights, the dead
        landscape of my forefathers and humming
        caravans in the night. They have built a car
        beneath my bed and sent me

        home along the anise path
        of airport beacons flashing
        thick armies into the dark. I grew up here. Fairview

        Cinema. The six
        point eight hit in the middle
        of the Sergeant Pepper movie. Everyone flooded
        out into the swinging

        lampposts, the ground was rolling
        about six feet under. So much motion! I couldn't wait

for the next quake along
Camino del Sur where we made this road
the route "del Surf" when I stood

on Colleen's shoulders
and painted a white "F" on the sign. Three
blocks away there was still the sea and laughed
and laughed till the waves rolled home. I think I
recognize my mother

Mrs. His-this driving me toward the fishing

boat at dawn. Stoplight. There's a trap
door at the bottom of the sea floor—Is that floor in motion
a notion of pleasure? Is this abstract

pleasurable? Is
concrete? Cream? Sublime

tries. What
is this? Time.

When the body arose
like a cloud unfolding

       It is good that you came,
       Newborn sky

Chiefest lamp of all the Earth, ethereal, bodily

And you, self-magnifying sons & daughters of Earth-
quake

the rolling genius of that laughing language
able to shake

boulders and dirt
Swirl, swirl

Sikelianos, it is reported

lived beyond the old borders of glaciers
                    in lovely blue roughly
            in the direction of alpha Gem
                        toward which
                the sun is moving
                            bird-caged
like you
            a comet had a head
            of dirty ice

            those speeding mountains
            of filthy water   knitting   interstellar   streams

When we were condensed out of clouds of dust, dust-devils made us as such
intricate, such dusky, throaty dust

All praise to the letter "dust"
Let the bod from the bodies
shine free

with the things I walked into the room with (animal
symmetry) (Not fifty miles of elbow room)
To stand apart from institutions

distorted utopias here on Earth

What do I have in common with my fellow humans?

I dream the dream of the animals dreaming
their rise and demise   Rise again

on the blond vapor that you were bathed in

Sunlight birthed us, & the smudge of our shadows

like a smooth moon of blackened stone
        the curves, rounds, body
        smelling of new-sanded wood

        shoulder, road along the coast, a cliff
        drops off precipitous
        an elbow, knee, hip, what
        one can burnish with one's hands in the night

The lines of the body are polished
by palms   or the imagination   or genes   (curve of the foot)

Cilia, spirochete, composite beings
        born of symbiont meetings
(humans) fall apart   Are you speaking of molecules
or community interactions?   I'm speaking here
only of the heart.

            My less fragile

body, little planet, had an answer, had
a question and response; an orbit offering an image

of all our circling grandstand

in a history of dark flickering between dawns, clusters
of nights and the days
between them

in the united states of all this place, every
amalgamated rock & singing string & dirt, our sexual
       flowering earth, vectee crowded
       with vectors. What
       have you made
       flower?
              anther
              anthem
              atom

Little planet, crystal ball
tells the tale of a many-layered dustcake

        From an ending star, iron becomes the dust that clumps to make a solid planet

As seen from afar:
mirrored tufty, spinning
pellet. Close under
our feet, our cloudy reflections
cast down
underground—

when the body
melts back into shadow, beginning
with the toes

and the dead adhere to the bed
where the beds are buried
with obsidian blades,
those wet beliefs
in bogs and on peaks.   We carried her body through the dark

deep in the days of human endeavor in grass boots

after dust caused men & women to come forth from ants
and learned a man's, a woman's, hands to resonate depth

Who do you love more,
bizarre   bird-and-flower, dust
or our heavenly wolf star?
Me,
or money?

In the dream it was
raining in the violet-tinged West. Who is
the hero in
this dream? The
cracks in the earth, reflective
pools of
blood reflecting
a ground reality, the foot-brings
of a snake. You were
warned of insects. Please
"believe me, there are things
you cannot write," the vacuum of space-time outside
the body, the
infinitely curving
body in alien
hours; "A small dark & trembling tree
is able to reassemble the
qualities of wind within
its leaves," anonymous stars do amalgamous yoga through the trees. Lie down with me, in all
the theories of earth arising from dirt. I am not the leopard lady who lived in the house before us on Garden Street,
leaping from counter to counter, banking off rafts of dark grammar. I am not La Llorona, la Malinche, weeping in
creeks for children she slaughtered. I don't mean a pool of blood, I mean a *pool* of *blood*, glassy and reflective over
the surface of the state, where any backyard pool should be; you can see airplanes pass over their bodies you see
them flitting and sliding, dragging across pools of blood. Now, the spoils, a collision
between history my enemy
and the self, as the future rearranges
the past I walk by the lake, "because I think the lake
is better than me"

Endangered, Threatened, & Extinct[xxv] *Interlude*
+
Outdoor Hazards

California Grizzly Bear EXTINCT **(1925) /** Point Arena Mountain Beaver / Sierra Nevada Red Fox /
Southern California Kit Fox EXTINCT **(1903) /** San Joaquin Kit Fox / Island Fox / **Giant Deer Mouse** EXTINCT
(1870) / Pacific Pocket Mouse / Salt-marsh Harvest Mouse / Southern Sea Otter / Riparian Brush Rabbit / Fresno
Kangaroo Rat / Giant Kangaroo Rat / Morro Bay Kangaroo Rat / San Bernadino Kangaroo Rat / Stephens' Kangaroo
Rat / Tipton Kangaroo Rat / Guadalupe Fur Seal / Steller Sea Lion / California Bighorn Sheep / Peninsular Bighorn
Sheep / Buena Vista Lake Shrew / San Joaquin Antelope Squirrel / Mohave Ground Squirrel / Amargosa Vole / Blue
Whale / Finback Whale / Gray Whale DELISTED (1994) / Humpback Whale / Right Whale / Sei Whale / Sperm
Whale / Wolverine / Riparian Woodrat

Short-tailed Albatross / California Condor / Greater Sandhill Crane / Western Yellow-billed Cuckoo / Bald Eagle /
American Peregrine Falcon DELISTED (1999) / Arctic Peregrine Falcon DELISTED (1994) / Gilded Northern Flicker /
Willow Flycatcher / Southwestern Willow Flycatcher / Coastal California Gnatcatcher / Aleutian Canada Goose
DELISTED (2001) / Swainson's Hawk / Marbled Murrelet / Great Gray Owl / Northern Spotted Owl / Elf Owl /
California Brown Pelican / Mountain Plover / Western Snowy Plover / California Black Rail / California Clapper
Rail / Light-footed Clapper Rail / Yuma Clapper Rail / San Clemente Loggerhead Shrike / **Santa Barbara Song
Sparrow** EXTINCT **(1967) /** Belding's Savannah Sparrow / San Clemente Sage Sparrow / Bank Swallow / California
Least Tern / Inyo California Towhee / Arizona Bell's Vireo / Least Bell's Vireo / Gila Woodpecker / **San Clemente
Bewick's Wren** EXTINCT **(1927)**

California Red-legged Frog / Southern California Yellow-legged Mountain Frog / Santa Barbara County California Tiger Salamander / Desert Slender Salamander / Kern Canyon Slender Salamander / Limestone Salamander / Santa Cruz Long-toed Salamander / Shasta Salamander / Siskiyou Mountains Salamander / Tehachapi Slender Salamander / Black Toad / Southwestern Arroyo Toad

Bonytail / **Thicktail Chub** EXTINCT (1980) / Tidewater Goby / Cottonball Marsh Pupfish / Desert Pupfish / Owens Pupfish / **Tecopa Pupfish** EXTINCT / **Shoshone Pupfish** EXTINCT / California Coastal Chinook Salmon ESU [4] / Spring-run Chinook Salmon ESU / Winter-run Chinook Salmon ESU / Central California Coho Salmon ESU / So. Oregon–No. California Coho Salmon ESU / Rough Sculpin / Delta Smelt / Sacramento Splittail (= Colorado Pikeminnow) / Northern California Steelhead ESU / Central California Coast Steelhead ESU / South-Central California Coast Steelhead ESU / Central Valley Steelhead ESU / Unarmored Threespine Stickleback / Lost River Sucker / Modoc Sucker / Razorback Sucker / Santa Ana Sucker / Shortnose Sucker / Bull Trout / Lahontan Cutthroat Trout / Little Kern Golden Trout / Paiute Cutthroat Trout / Cowhead Lake Tui Chub / Mohave Tui Chub / Owens Tui Chub

Southern Rubber Boa / Barefoot Banded Gecko / Blunt-nosed Leopard Lizard / Coachella Valley Fringe-toed Lizard / Island Night Lizard / Green Sea Turtle / Leatherback Sea Turtle / Loggerhead Sea Turtle / Olive Ridley Sea Turtle / Giant Garter Snake / San Francisco Garter Snake / Alameda Striped Racer (Alameda Whipsnake) / Desert Tortoise

White Abalone / Morro Shoulderband (Banded Dune) Snail / Trinity Bristle Snail / Shasta (Placid) Crayfish / Conservancy Fairy Shrimp / Longhorn Fairy Shrimp / Riverside Fairy Shrimp / San Diego Fairy Shrimp / Vernal Pool Fairy Shrimp / Vernal Pool Tadpole Shrimp / California Freshwater Shrimp

Delta Green Ground Beetle / **Dohrn's Elegant Eucremid Beetle** EXTINCT / **Mono Lake Hyogrotus Beetle** EXTINCT / Mount Hermon June Beetle / Ohlone Tiger Beetle / Valley Elderberry Longhorn Beetle / Bay Checkerspot Butterfly / Behren's Silverspot Butterfly / Callippe Silverspot Butterfly / El Segundo Blue Butterfly / Lange's Metalmark Butterfly / Lotis Blue Butterfly / Mission Blue Butterfly / Myrtle's Silverspot Butterfly / Oregon Silverspot Butterfly / Palos Verdes Blue Butterfly / San Bruno Elfin Butterfly / Smith's Blue Butterfly / **Xerxes Blue Butterfly** EXTINCT / Quino Checkerspot / **Castle Lake Caddisfly** EXTINCT / **King's Creek Parapsyche Caddisfly** EXTINCT / Delhi Sands Flower-loving Fly / **Valley Mydas Fly** EXTINCT / *Volutine stonemyian tabanid* **fly** EXTINCT

[4] Ecologically Significant Unit

/ Zayante Band-winged Grasshopper / **Antioch Dunes Shieldback Katydid** EXTINCT / **Antioch Cophuran Robberfly** EXTINCT / Kern Primrose Sphinx Moth / Laguna Mountains Skipper / *Mesocapnia bakeri* **Stonefly** EXTINCT / **Antioch Mutillid Wasp** EXTINCT / **Antioch Sphecid Wasp** EXTINCT / **Yorba Linda Trigonoscuta Weevil** EXTINCT / **Fort Ross Trigonoscuta Weevil** EXTINCT[5][xxvi]

Outdoor Hazards

There have been six fatal mountain lion attacks on humans in California since 1890. Between 1907 and 1950, 10,588 bountied[6] mountain lions were killed in California. From 1898 to 1997, 53 people were attacked by coyotes. One person has been killed by coyotes in recorded U.S. history. Twenty-four died in helicopter crashes and other accidents while trying to kill coyotes in a federal management program (1983–2000). There were 835 hunting-related injuries in the U.S in the year 2000. There were 91 hunting-related deaths (deemed accidental) that year. In seventeen years (1979–1996), there were 30 dog-bite related fatalities in California. Nationwide dog-bite related fatalities in that same period were 304+. The average number of annually reported dog bites in U.S.: 4 million. There have been 101 shark attacks in California in the past 77 years (74% by Great Whites). Nine of those were fatal. In 2001, 6,516 Californians were killed in car crashes; the number injured that year was 413,913. The leading cause of crashes: fiddling with "carcooning" devices, such as cell phones, in-car VCRs and electronics or radio-CD systems.

The Pyramid of Numbers

On twenty square miles of brushland there will be enough insects to feed 100,000 white-footed mice, and many birds. There will be enough mice and birds to feed 18 foxes, and one pair of Golden Eagles. How much needed for a single cougar? (Unknown.)

5 This list does not include the 218 state-listed species and subspecies of rare, threatened, and endangered plants.
   (The California Native Plants Society puts the number closer to 1,000. They currently list 28 extinct California plant species.)

6 In a state-run program of extermination (run, as noted, till 1950), bounty was $20 per hide, later $30 for females.

Animals of Prey (Federalized Extermination, 1914/15 Congressional Act; the Cooper's Hawk "a species to be destroyed")

After they had killed the hawks, raptors, cougars, coyotes, wolves, the bobcats, and grizzlies,[7] one night in the oil town of Taft 100 million house mice advanced. They "invaded beds and nibbled the hair of . . . sleepers, chewed through the sides of wooden storehouses to get at food . . . and crawled . . . into children's desks at Conley School."

> Advancing to the southwest, mice killed a sheep and devoured its carcass in less than a day. A column slipped past poison-filled trenches to touch off an exodus of women from Ford City . . . Another column captured the Petroleum Club golf course after token opposition from fleeing golfers. To the north, hordes swarmed over the Taft-Bakersfield Highway, where thousands were ground to death under car wheels, making the highway dangerously slippery.[xxvii]

"At first local authorities tried to destroy the advancing rodent hordes with mechanical harvesters, but the blades 'became choked with fur, flesh, and blood to the resemblance of a sausage mill.'"

---

7 One animal control officer in San Bernadino estimated that he alone had personally destroyed 10,000 predatory animals (Mike Davis, *Ecology of Fear*).

Blow-out on Platform A

Every living thing lies in one of two
or three Kingdoms—so
where do the rest of us
go?

This poem is about making good
on Linnaeus's crazy world where

I'm worried for the cyberphyla . . .
which is why I
kneel among the lesser deuterostomes
licking an *Anthopleura elegantissima* & all
the radiate animals

lay my head among
foredune & dune scrub & dune swale
& foreshadow & shadowplay, fore-
play in bushes
amidst ancient assemblages of organisms, give head to
armored stink bugs, decapods & pinnipeds

It was a Californian; I was. I can call myself
a Californian because
I was there in the state of the Sisters
of Perpetual Indulgence

"I saw the red Pacific Electric
city trains dismantled & replaced (L.A.) by
automative freeways, saw
the orange bulldoze, 'Dad,
are we real?'" "we slide our
barques . . . past burning parts, ports of
barbecues, seized women, farewell to the flesh
and fleas in a new vehicle 'driving . . . vast
distances to . . .'   roadside attractions, snake
farms, jelly stands with curios outside Palm City" no truck with sexual samadhi
of Mickey screaming terror
& bright delight when I drop
darkness hell of Space
into dizzy Disney with spines in the dorsal;
pickled tatters, distorted flashes
of eel-grass in a completely objective destructed Sea of Cortez

What the little dangers what the large   What medicines will be
needed, collecting   California in the littoral

What was
indicated on the tide charts
under bridges, in bays, in North Beach
Chinatown, what was writ
in water, under wharves with
mussels clinging by *byssus* threads, stringy
grit-filled frilly girl lips ("The orange flesh of this mussel makes fine
        fish bait and is also excellent as human food")

An escaped moon pit
over the anomalous orbit of Pluto
tipped at 17° to the solar plane

cannot explain. They *have* divided the water
into districts, clouds running strangling patterns over the surface, bridges
cut the bay at key points: navel, heart; my language is rippled word
by word by human
crowding

What activities of the land are there
        to believe in?
        "road-building, brick laying," filling
        gas tanks, cans with sardines, cash at dawn, what my
        wife has planted outside of where I have
        to get to. Fisher's 3-volume starfish homily mono-
        graph lashed to a rail of the deckhouse.

The subtle lives unwind
unsubtly below
airplanes & sober cloud

cover   Little patches of snow
get icy, big patches pit themselves
against the sun, melt slowly, slowly become
rags of snow again, the
quiet clouds continue to
move their cords silently overhead, under
the pulleys & ropes, break up (a streak
of sun, the snow melts intelligently, the
clouds must knit up again);
more snow, the slow
lives move safely, unsafe
through Fort Dodge, dumb
Minneapolis, Lake
Michigan, Idaho, scattered
clouds a soft geology, Tahoe, Lakes
gather themselves
up to form
nervous revolutions revolutionary
lakes fold up and set themselves down blankety and thirsty, thirsty people
wade through them, "the lines ruled lines never stop,
a pleasure, the way the lines separate one
from another Ohio Indiana Kansas Nebraska Tennessee from Alabama
straight lines" go to ask all over nothing neat
and clean but a next and a heat there like a map of Americas
"You never feel it in a car you
may see a sign but you will not feel
that you have crossed a line Louisiana Iowa Idaho" a poem
of all contiguous noncontiguous states

"That you can make a car go
they take for granted, that you
make it stop & go & turn

around they take for granted
So those are the things I carry in my pocket, the Ranch &
the permission to drive
in California"

Now it's just slag heap babies, muddy & blech & scrubby snow
But if there's no acid in that lake, I'll live here
over that lake
35,000 feet in the air
If there's no oxygen
I'll leave
If there are a set of
[clear][able] instructions I'd like to invite my human & animal
vegetable, even, & mineral friends
California Minnesota New York
slide out
over the gray world
the just-no-solutions one
the if you want to step outside
carbon stinking up the tracks, black
        gravel-gutted
Hey, wait a minute, it *is* night
No it's not
I know, I know, it's night / not-night
It's the rolling earth
with its ass on fire

⊰

"It is a rule in paleontology that ornamentation and complication precede extinction"
and nothing we say or think can stop it

My goal is to relate the descriptions to living animals
    Who is truly flea-bitten here? on hills hanging over beaches thatched
with reticent brush, the yellow intensities shining on cliffs, and below, it's
riffled with blue. Which animal?

A heady crazy mirage starts up to distort the land
Islands rise where they are not, concealed rocks
float like dark shadows; the discoverers arrive
on stilts, in high masks, in the rush of collecting
Sand crabs witness to the holy rubble tribunal
little tribal crabs in masks of bryozoa, algae, a budding hydra's bright disguising hosiery

"The many-formed personality phases of history shuffle," a jackknife clam changes to fit the new shape, but with
lumps and corners; the rise & fall of riches in family lines;

Do I have a clear picture of my field?

The picture is wide & colored & varied [beautiful]
with strength & energy of mind, "the tide pool stretches
both ways back
to homunculus and leaping out toward Pluto"
fossil echinoderms & evolutional series thrust
        "toward death and renewal";

In this horology, "twist the tide pool and the stars into the pattern of paleontology and time"

They told me to put   I'm putting these peaches into this Arizona
desert basement where they will ripen in two years' time; for here in this upper California
market, there is no room.

Houses falling into clay
Cliff houses where we do our fingerpaint fall down into sand and clay
Houses falling from the sky
and people in them, whole families, ready-made and settling
into California clay & canyons
And fathers who sell houses falling into clay and mothers who sell them

In this house, the one I live in, *The California Papers* is shelved next to *The Pennywhistle Primer*

The closed system of the ocean opens before us, its
emotional content rising up in precipitous belief

—That's stupid. What does the ocean believe in? In time-place
truths, when applied or if applicable
to many seas? the residua to maintain races
of rare or common species; the spell
of light canopying; the speed of it "conspiring"; of the stony corals, the Orange Cup's
walls of jagged skeleton; of rocks shot through with Buckshot
Barnacles? The scatterbrained Solitary Green Anemone throws venomous harpoon cysts at a stone; stepping not
on stone but onto the yielding bodies
of Aggregate Anemones; I too want a fantastic tentacular crown; yet try licking an anemone
and it will sting;

Slipping down to the beach at night to sleep under the whipping
coats of catamarans—No fear but that the tides would rise
against our feet

Stepping back into the blank apartment, faded dizzy sun-print on the eyes
Spirits of trembling daisies boom forth for our dark & seriously heliographic ears

Had we heard of that arching spiral, the upward panic
like huge goblets of water dropped
into the Pacific vat and radiating outward?

Hoary mollusks lie in wait for their Cambrian prey
            ready with radula to
                        rasp and bore

Winds from the North, winds
from the South, Chinook
was such a dog, a Chow, who fell off a ship

In the last of the days of the Spoon-faced Nematodes

Remember those days I was picked up by a wave and ground into the substrate
            & like the lugworm, swallowed sand
Remember the low-flying helicopters we used to moon

        The concept-cool kitchen tile floor of California

        Eating medjools in the shade
                of drive-in swapmeet date palms, ransacking
                the scattered lit. of marine invertebrates

The orange's membrane half-swallowed, pulled
              back from the throat to be chewed again

In the great annals of the Annelids, secrets
              of natural selection in Polychaetes

Remember a member of a ready-made (Stella) trying to kiss you in the night
              because she thought you were her boyfriend Wayne
                        or Brett but you were just two girls in bed

              J.S. harpooning stingrays mid-coitus
              The volume and shape of water in Bays

In the final hour of the fingered limpet, the whorled dogwinkle

              the double-edged pebbles, rocky berth of our Haskells "Hilton"
                        (the pebbles and rocks are gone)
Remember the brothers Brian and Brett gunned down on a beach in La Paz

              If I could just get over those mountains to the West
                        where are stone azurite wings of the Beechey Jay
                  jaguarundi, leoncillo, ocelot, tigrillo, secretive cats of low quavering

Jumping off piers into the snap of the stunning water, saying
              our fucking-A's on the cliff

Remember Tina's head crushed in
                        where her forehead smashed into asphalt
the roughly transparent night runs
              a trance like iron-ink   she lies
                        quite young, quite dead, "disremembering
                                  that sweet land": sleep

We held our flashlights over the surface of the water
Sea bottom alive with invertebrates
Isopods and mysids come swarming to the illuminating circles
Colonies of tunicates have taken shapes like fingers

The tree-frog in the high pool in the mountain cleft thinking   This is the pool where I nearly
        drowned swinging out on the rope against that greenery

Sleeping under crags in
the odor of the cooling earth
And quiet racer snakes in the cold water

In some summers we may walk the beach with our feet
        higher than our heads
The intertidal zone and its contiguous waters which taught me what I know about fishes
        is alternating air and water: All water
will want to return to the sea
with its corroded chemical cargo of "practically everything"

OCEANS   TRADE BODIES

vast sheet a thin skin; deeper

                             bioluminescent life forms under heavy pressure, sea-
                             floor communities at hot tectonic edges
gigantic red-tipped beardworms chew chemosynthesized bacteria, creatures
independent

of the
Sun

Dead bodies throw trace
elements: mollusks concentrate
on copper, radiolarians do strontium, Earth accelerates

Ocean waves are born in storms and travel
        to farther shores

The term *sea* is used when waves have no pattern, the surface
        is confused

Tell us tales of the magic numbers by which waves move. Some say every seventh
wave is big, others the ninth; any surfer knows
the nine by nine is the wave worth
waiting for.

A train of waves arrives on shore, met
by some other train from some other storm in some

other sea. Two trains meet mid-crest, they kiss; and the swell is high. If a wave "feels the bottom"
in all its particles and motion it will
break.

Undertow. Riptide. A current pulls your feet toward open sea.

Headlands draw waves
headless over passing waters. Sand disappears
into dunes, canyons, breakwaters, beaches denuded, what

decomposes there "cannot be cut with a burnt stick at night"
Soon to be used by the sea, I
break the waves but leave plenty

of water for you

You, "the result of some hydrographic accident"

This is "the press of the redstart hand," the "float and odor
                                        of hair"

The drag and purpose of the purple jelly's bell, *Velella velella* By-the-Wind Sailor in pint-
            sized plastic sails drifts
Limpets & periwinkles hold their breath
            till surf rides in; tidal
            creatures scuttle
            for cover, drawn in

            to webs of radiowave and powerport

Neaptides, springtides   Sun & Moon canceling each other out or augmenting the other's
activities and argument

Resonance & reflection within the trembling waters as they shake and giggle in any
body   beautifully advancing

fogbank like a wall of
natural wonder to lock us in

And of those who themselves sank in the sea

And in the shadows of the night approached we
opulent stars, as suggested
by Virgil

Just as the Sun's
profession is not
to turn, our bright
burning star
so, driving my car
into medians, smashing up
volkswagens, burying the thought
in the flesh (the will may have no limits
but there is the matter,
friends), the dead-black

waters of the underworld in California
"the region of the shades, & sleep,
& drowsy night," like
a leaky coracle
floating on this marshy crack called Earth

Were the sensitive places discovered yet?—"ball of thumb, ear-lobe, skin below the ribs, thigh and lip"
"and smell of reptiles" and smell of sex "and smell of death"   No, no, no

It was the days of sweet fuck-all
No grim cheerleader for hot sauce behind the counter

but igniting spongy aborescences in the evening trees
and grunion runs at high-tide nights, the silverside animals flashing in great heaps on the beach

the water's surface talks back to waves in scaly
(windswept) shapes, & the sea shows us
micro monsters caught
in writhing waves, aspiring
to wrest themselves free
of rock
bottom
shore or
sea

(I dream it
as if I were the sea, adamant, sea's
big muscle
squeezing me)

nudibranch or sea-
millipede dressed to match
the evening sun, every
leg (shape
of a question mark) shuffling
sea

ghost shrimp
pounds on a gastropod's trap
door, spiny fish nibble toes, crab
eats crab, some scrap of purple
flesh flutters in currents; here

as in every tidepool, a minute-by-minute it-
could-be-curtains

knots up around us—
Akilah's son, Judy's sister,
my father; soldiers and civilians
tonight; tonight
the net will tighten

around some-
one;   Let it
not be me
or someone
I love, let it
not be any
animal
rock
or sea   Let it
flow on
between itself
life : death : life : death

To sun gives we add
    light[xxviii]

To shaggy we add
    sun

                        its light
like a fly buzzing round my wrist, individual
        wings &
        what things
            light likes

                sloppy hills
                        at dusk

To map lies we add
    in dust

find the desert spot
        where dirt gives way
            to sand

the slow parade of land
beneath our feet   cliff
    faces bitten
away by wind, see
Own Face there
cracked wash

soft

Spring wears
material of elegance

Summer, sessile, is wearing
thinner What shall I
now what

pursue now
what peruse with undivided focus in the froth

of the present?

Shadows move through our mouths. Bushes
hang in the indirect air, when will they explode, and where

cliffs are migrating slowly south
or to the north, the ocean is, and ice
caps and mountains grow smaller, carp move dusking
through frigid waters.   All the quadrupeds amidst the stucco

do not bring tokens to the subway, "they do not lie awake in the dark" thinking; the placid
opossum trundles naked and blind
across freeways where cars full of minute wickednesses
speed. And bays are
dredged, "cranes carry mudflats
forward into air and time," the planet

representing planets will crackle

and spit. Pismo's tars forgive
the typographical errors[xxix] of the beach. I will spend my weeks

with a metal detector combing the sands for silver dollars

and in the rufus hours of evening, looking for the Little Heart Shell,
lie down in the quiet waters and fold myself

into the cunning jewel box of the Agate Chama, "elbows
in sea-gaps," clinging to acony, of brittle and white, and bury

my arms
& legs in the earth at this
juncture;

Radiographs

the only form
above the moon

And below it
the stubborn softly-lit grasses

And evening
in rubified clamour, everything rubiginous & rotating
in horizontal & vertical layers
of green for meadows, blue for seas
green for mountains, blue for creeks
black for rocks
blue for
green
ruby for ruby-
crack,

glass

shards in the alley outside my window. Outside my window, the homicides which did not take place
& maybe a body out there by the train tracks
swimming off the Pacific's cunning subterranean tiled abyss
and never touch bottom

California   keep
on, beneficent
as the sun and sea, I ask you leave
to roll on the first inch

of its shady territory; I believe a hundred dollars
and a year would support me   in California
The rest I would pluck from the avocado & lemon tree & the sea

where there is no heavy snow but it is "raining behind my back . . . [and] your rain
will be my rain," in the discovery of apposites that are not bicoastal

California utterly more sky of the looking everything in the mouth of tidelines
the tip of the snail's horn caught in the eye & ice plant poppy bright by the highway deeps

of bituminous, "how do I notice
while being Am, am reading the rocks
noting and riding the surface" my arm rising
out of the dead ring
                    with rain
         over the
veering
Earth.

Endnotes

i   in the east, might they think
an echinoderm is a series
of snowflakes, one
piled up to the next

in the west, it's that plum
that is not a word, it's something you eat, it's full
of design

ii   All sparrows' songs,
             granites, grasses, collaborate, language
is a shape
the planet takes.

[poem in which the planet takes over]

iii   An *asteroidea* (starfish) begins as a bilateral entity, but does
not stay obsessed with mirrors, mirror stages, self-reflec-
tion, binary modes.

iv   the ghostly shroud around a cell
[: the *Laspeyresia saltitans* moth lays her egg
    in the flower and around that flower a seedpod is
fashioned]

v   I'd like to encourage that fog in a hurry over hills
                 tangling up manzanita & madrone
                       to help me find me
                      shadowed under clicking oaks

vi   "Breeding habits of the Native Oyster involve a series of
successive alternations in sex, each individual changing
from male to female and back again several times during
its lifetime. Some of those in the process of changing may
be fully functioning hermaphrodites, operating for a short
time as both male and female" (Sam Hinton, *Seashore Life
of Southern California: An Introduction to the Animal Life of
California Beaches South of Santa Barbara*).

vii   I stole $25 worth of silver quarters from Mrs. Oscar Mayer
(of the wiener fortune), where my mother was a maid, by
hiding them in my mouth. (It was at her house that I first
encountered canapés, though not the word.) I was made
to give the quarters back, but was allowed to do so with-
out telling Mrs. Mayer what I had done.

viii   Significant Ecological Area (SEA)

ix   a.k.a. Walter Nordhoff

x   anticipating the next California   will they
make me eat
the chemical snowflakes?

xi   I once saw a caged leoncillo outside Tucson, Arizona
which had just killed and eaten a bird that had flown
through its small compound. Minutes after, the only evi-
dence of this delicately performed operation was one
feather on the ground near the leoncillo's forepaw, and on
the fur of its lower lip a tiny, ruby-like drop of blood.

xii   "The abandonment and destruction of property here—at
Deer Creek, is extraordinary . . ."

"I took advantage of the piles of bacon . . . , and had all
mine trimmed of fat and the rusty exterior and the requi-
site amount of pounds replaced by choice cuts from the
abandoned piles. Was told of a man here, who a few days
ago offered a barrel of sugar for sale, for about threble its
cost, price—and unable to obtain that, he poured Spirits

of turpentine on it, and burnt it up. The spirit of selfishness has been here beautifully developed . . ."
(J. Goldsborough Bruff, *Gold Rush*).

xiii   "While wintering on the island La Posesión, [San Miguel] on January 3, 1543, Juan Rodriguez, captain of these ships [San Salvador and Victoria], departed this life from a fall he had at this [same] island" on the way up the coast. Cabrillo, who had marched on Mexico City with Cortés, died of a gangrenous broken arm (some reports say leg) and was most likely buried on *tuqan* / La Posesión / San Miguel island, which his crew renamed Juan Rodriguez Island, a name that did not stick.

xiv   There are currently efforts underway to revive the Chumash language. Santa Ynez Chumash Reservation population = 320; Americans of Chumash descent: ≈ 3,000 – 5,000.

xv   "art's lower limit: actual life, a condition of savagery" (Frye)

". . . one Sunday afternoon I wandered out along the Desplaines River / and saw a crowd of Hungarians under the trees with their women and children and a keg of beer and an accordion." (Sandburg, "Happiness")

xvi   I promise to stay and watch till the last arrowed sparrow goes past.

xvii   Field Note:

bull thistle

chufa sedge spikelet
hottentot fig: ice plant brought in to bite erosion

Jewelweed: (California) Dodder

a.k.a. strangleweed, devil's guts, goldthread, pull-down devil's-ringlets, hellbine, devil's-hair, hairweed, the (chlorophyll-lacking) Love-vine that twines around its
   host & sucks
on goldenrod, potato, smartweed . . .
what is the gene sequence in its springtime corolla?
a seed sleeps for five years, planning an attack on alfalfa
   native contraceptive, baths for tuberculars &
   fevered children, a Chinese eye-wash, an anti-inflammatory

xviii   Of Phylum Echinodermata (Starfish, Brittle Stars, Sea Urchins, Sand Dollars): "although the larvae start life in bilaterally symmetrical form (with a mirror-image on each side of an imaginary longitudinal midline), the adults of most species attain a radial symmetry . . . around a common center point . . . which in this phylum is based on a plan of five" (Hinton, *Seashore Life of Southern California*).

xix   Why did I watch *Jaws* three times in a row then go swimming at midnight? This changed the way I felt about the ocean later. Sharks-tooth necklaces: wore their triangular serrated white teeth on fragile silver chains around my neck.

xx   To consider:
a starfish's utilitarian
notion of gonads & ampullae. Can I be the discoverer
of the glorified form & function of sea stars? Sea stars
   are. Can I be
      the tapering rays & central discs, yellow
      / orange arms, heavenly body for blue
      sharks to chomp upon? Sea stars
      are.

xxi our highways & hiking trails built on anterior trade routes
& footpaths

xxii From a dream in which the movie that was screening
across the dreamscape was haunted by a dead, jealous
actress (Carole Lombard by name). She is haunting Clark
Gable and another leading lady, interrupting the film with
tear-streaked luminous black & white visage—screaming,
crying, threatening every time certain scenes appear, till
finally she axes Gable and the offending lady. Because it is a
film, replicable in time (a virus splicing memory), this
ghost can haunt the scenes that trouble her again and
again, an undigitized glitch in the screening. Old curving
cars gun down a rain-filled mainstreet, and Lombard's
ghost appears and murders Gable and his co-star again and
again. Sitting in the dark theater, we are traumatized by
this celluloid haint.

xxiii "This so alarmed the [Chumash] that . . . [many] departed
and were settled in bands of three or four hundred in the
several missions," where many did not survive (H. W.
Henshaw, in *Anthropological Records, California Linguistic
Records,* v. 15, no. 2, from an interview with Anisetto
Pajilacheet in 1884). Santa Rosa (*wi'ma* [Redwood]) Island,
which the Indians reached in seagoing canoes, was one of
the last outposts for the Chumash. San Nicolas, however,
was the Island of the Blue Dolphins, made famous by the
story of Karana, a 12-year old Chumash girl who was
stranded alone on the island for 18 years when all her
people left.
www.crustal.uscb.edu/ics/sb_eqs/1912/chumash.html.

xxiv Gin Chow, a Chinese immigrant to Santa Barbara, famous
for weather predictions. Published *Gin Chow's First Annual
Almanac* in 1932. "His record for accuracy was uncanny.
He predicted the 1923 earthquake in Yokohama . . . [I]n
1923 . . . he announced that on June 29, two years later,

Santa Barbara would be visited by a major earthquake"
(T. M. Storke, editor of the *Santa Barbara News-Press* in
1925, from *California Editor,* Westernlore Press, 1958, Los
Angeles). www.crustal.uscb.edu/ics/sb_eqs/1925/ chow.html.

xxv This list only includes species found in California; there
are over 1700 species noted on the larger Federal List.
This list was drawn from www.dfg.ca.gov/hcpb/species/t_
e_spp/tespp.shtml, which was updated May 5, 2003. Note
that animals are sometimes "delisted" because populations
have recovered, sometimes because the species has gone
extinct.

xxvi A few weedy species that are opportunistic, thriving in
California: coyotes opossums skunks squirrels rac-
coons jays humans red-eared slider turtles African
(Killer) bees

xxvii William Rintoul, "How the West Side Boomed," *Guidebook:
Geology and Oil Fields, West Side Southern San Joaquin Valley,*
as quoted by Mike Davis, *Ecology of Fear.*

xxviii
                                        this landscape
                            is time's elaboration, and time
                                    has something to do
                            with eternity's ideas, too

". . . into eternity of which this vegetable world is but a
shadow. Hold to the now, the here, through which all
future plunges to the past." —JJ

xxix *Coquilles*—Fr.: shells; typos.

Key

JA   John Adams (composer)
WB   Walter Benjamin
RWE   Ralph Waldo Emerson
FH   Fanny Howe
JJ   James Joyce
WW   Walt Whitman
WCW William Carlos Williams

Further Acknowledgments

A number of texts were instrumental over the course of the seven years it took to write this poem. A partial list would include:

Edward F. Ricketts' and John Steinbeck's collaborative *The Log from the Sea of Cortez* (early and key); Sam Hinton's *Seashore Life of Southern California,* with his fabulous drawings; *Between Pacific Tides* (a study of the flora and fauna in the Pacific intertidal zone, by Ricketts, et al.); *Integrated Principles of Zoology; December's Child: A Book of Chumash Oral Narratives,* from the collections by J. P. Harrington; Mike Davis's *Ecology of Fear;* an outdated and funny *Introduction to the Natural History of Southern California; The Sibley Guide to Birds;* Kevin Starr's *Americans and the California Dream: 1850–1915; California Heritage;* and John McPhee's *Assembling California.*

Two lectures, one by Richard Serra at Princeton University, and another by Peter Warshall at Naropa University (see the recently published *Civil Disobediences),* also provided inspiration.

A Note on the Type

One of the private pleasures of book designers is to select typefaces that allude in some way to the text, or to the author's personal heritage. In this book, we have selected a type for the text that alludes to the subject of this book, and a display face that harks back to our author's roots.

Frederick W. Goudy designed the type used for the text in this book in 1938 for the University of California Press, to be used exclusively by the press as a "proprietary" typeface. His goal, as he stated in his book, *Goudy's Type Designs,* was "to give to it the utmost distinction compatible with its purpose" while striving "for the greatest legibility possible." Dubbed University of California Old Style, it was first used for *Typologia,* a book on the history of type design, written for the press by Goudy, and published in 1940 to coincide with a celebration of the 500th anniversary of Gutenberg's invention of movable type.

Monotype released this font in 1956 under the name Californian, and Tony Stan designed the ITC version seen here, under the name Berkeley.

Futura's form was inspired by ancient Greek letters, by Roman letterforms used in the tomb of the Scipios, and by classical revival architects in 18th century London. It was designed by Paul Renner in 1928 and reflected Bauhaus principles of perfect squares and isosceles triangles. It became the most popular san serif in the mid-20th century.

Image Credits

Palmier glorieux, painting, Isabelle Pelissier
Beach Scene, collage, Isabelle Pelissier
"It ended on the beach," cut up, Eleni Sikelianos
Path to the Sea, collage, Isabelle Pelissier
Hand Signals, drawing, Nancy Davidson
Points of Tension / Intersection, drawing, Nancy Davidson
Pseudo Oreaster, drawing, Nancy Davidson
Hand Signals, drawing, Nancy Davidson
Photo of the author, circa 1972
Plank Road, Highway 80, postcard, Merle Porter ("The Postcard King")
Parking Lot, collage, Isabelle Pelissier
Hand, drawing, Nancy Davidson
Whale Bones, Lorna Hunt
Hand Signals, drawing, Nancy Davidson
Car in Oak Tree, matchbox car in oak sapling, Peter Cole
Complicated Brody, drawing, Nancy Davidson
The Yucca, postcard, photographer unknown
Sleeping Lady with Spine, collage, Isabelle Pelissier
Lotus Feet, collage, Isabelle Pelissier
The Cyclone, photograph, Brenda Coultas
Devil's Golf Course, photograph, Bancroft Library
Earthquake Damage, Crack in Street, 1925, photograph, Bancroft Library
Mannequin parts from L.A. rubble, after the riots, Peter Cole
Palm Trees, photograph, Lorna Hunt

Funder Acknowledgment

Coffee House Press is an independent nonprofit literary publisher. Our books are made possible through the generous support of grants and gifts from many foundations, corporate giving programs, individuals, and through state and federal support. This project received major funding from the National Endowment for the Arts, a federal agency. Coffee House Press has also received support from the Minnesota State Arts Board, through an appropriation by the Minnesota State Legislature and by the National Endowment for the Arts; and from the Elmer and Eleanor Andersen Foundation; the Buuck Family Foundation; the Bush Foundation; the Grotto Foundation; the Lerner Family Foundation; the McKnight Foundation; the Outagamie Foundation; the John and Beverly Rollwagen Foundation; the law firm of Schwegman, Lundberg, Woessner & Kluth, P.A.; Target, Marshall Field's, and Mervyn's with support from the Target Foundation; James R. Thorpe Foundation; West Group; the Woessner Freeman Foundation; and many individual donors.

This activity is made possible in part by a grant from the Minnesota State Arts Board, through an appropriation by the Minnesota State Legislature and a grant from the National Endowment for the Arts.

MINNESOTA STATE ARTS BOARD

NATIONAL ENDOWMENT FOR THE ARTS

To you and our many readers across the country, we send our thanks for your continuing support.

Good books are brewing at coffeehousepress.org